West Coast Plays

Outstanding New Plays From The Coast

PUBLISHER

Robert Valine

EDITOR

Rick Foster

REGIONAL EDITORS

Richard Edwards, Seattle
Robert Eisele, Los Angeles
Edward Weingold, San Francisco

EDITORIAL ASSISTANTS

Ted Griggs
Edith Looney

West Coast Plays is published twice a year (Spring and Fall) in Berkeley, California. Subscriptions available at $10 per year. Send check or money order to West Coast Plays, P.O. Box 7206, Berkeley, CA 94707.

This project is supported by a grant from the National Endowment for the Arts in Washington, D.C., a Federal agency.

ISBN 0-934782-04-0

AVAILABLE

West Coast Plays 2 (Spring 1978)

Robert Gordon's *And*
Michael McClure's *Goethe: Ein Fragment*
Louis Phillips' *The Last of the Marx Brothers' Writers*
John Robinson's *Wolves*

West Coast Plays 3 (Fall 1978)

Robert Eisele's *Animals Are Passing from Our Lives*
Nicholas Kazan's *Safe House*
J. Paul Porter's *St. George*
Susan Rivers' *Maud Gonne Says No to the Poet*
William Whitehead's *And If That Mockingbird
        Don't Sing*

West Coast Plays 4 (Spring 1979)

Adele Edling Shank's *Sunset/Sunrise*
Ted Pezzulo's *Skaters*
Madeline Puccioni's *Two O'Clock Feeding*
Albert Innaurato's *Earth Worms*

Order from:
West Coast Plays
P.O. Box 7206
Berkeley, CA 94707

$4.95 each (add 6% sales tax in California)

Contents

The Playwrights

ROBERT PATRICK   (*Judas*)

Robert Patrick should need no introduction to the American public. He is the author of more plays than we could possibly list and his *Kennedy's Children* has been given hundreds of productions from Broadway to small bars. Patrick is liable to turn up at any theater anywhere in the country where new plays are being produced though his permanent address is in New York, where he has no phone, preferring to "use that $600 a month to take young actors to lunch."

LISA SHIPLEY   (*The Bathtub*)

Lisa Shipley graduated from the University of Washington School of Drama in 1978. Her recent works include *Dear Child,* presented at the New Womans Playwrights Festival, and *The Cat's Meow,* presented as part of the New Playwrights Forum at the Empty Space Theatre in Seattle. She is on the board of directors of The Womyn's Theatre.

NANCY LARSON   (*Imitations*)

Nancy Larson was born in Los Angeles in 1950 and grew up in Woonsocket, Rhode Island. She collaborated with actors in creating the play *Bad Conscience,* which was produced at the Odyssey Theater and La Mama, Los Angeles. She co-authored the screenplay *Parzival* and has adapted for the screen *The Wizard of Loneliness* and *The Tracker.*

MARTIN EPSTEIN   (*Autobiography of a Pearl Diver*)

Martin Epstein came to San Francisco from New York in the early sixties. He has taught literature, drama, and playwriting at San Francisco State University and other bastions of higher learning. He was an associate director with the San Francisco Actor's Workshop and later co-founded his own theater, Encounter. His play *Your Back Yard My Back Yard* was produced at the 1978 Bay Area Playwrights' Festival.

Judas
Robert Patrick

Judas was first performed by the Pacific Conservatory of the Performing Arts in Santa Maria, California. The production opened in April 1978 with the following cast:

PILATE	Laird Williamson
KLAUTUS	Peter Crook
HEROD	Cal Winn
JUDAS	Mark Harelik
MARY	Kathy Brady
JOSEPH	Richard Riehle
JESUS	David Williams
PETER	Anthony Henderson
UNDERSTUDY	Paul Mackley
FOLLOWERS OF JESUS	Paul Bates, John Becker, Bonnie A. Bowers, Alex Boyle, Jana Carson, Charles Craig, Claudia Golde, Lydia Hannibal, Scott Hart, Philip L. Jones, Moira Keefe, Kelly Kinzley, Ron Lindblom, Brian P. O'Moore, Jean Hickerson Paulson, Rachel Pauley, Anthony Powell, Lynne Powell, Kim Saxey, Brent Shaphren, Sally Smythe, Daria Sullivan, Joel Swetow, James Tyrone Wallace II, Stefan Windroth, Lynn Zwissler

Directed by Kent Paul
Designed by Patrice Miroballi
Costumes by John Dexter
Lighting by John Fernandez

Photos courtesy of Robert Patrick.

CHARACTERS

JUDAS: A young Jew, training for an executive position in the Roman Occupation Government. He is in his early twenties, intelligent, somewhat timid, wears suits, glasses.

KLAUTUS: A young Roman, athletic, pompous, "trig," condescending to most but eager to please his superior.

PILATE: A boyish aristocrat in his fifties, well-tailored, excitable, dramatic, passionately intellectual.

HEROD: The effete puppet-king of Judea. Wears a flashy uniform.

MARY: A Jewish housewife in her early fifties. She is dramatic, mercurial, forceful.

JOSEPH: Her husband, the same age. He is not so much cowed as confused by his wife. Wears stained work-clothes.

JESUS: Their son, early thirties. He is thin, tall, with commanding eyes. Wears "street-people" clothes. His thoughts express themselves instantly in his physical states. His hands and arms are eloquent and he has a superbly musical voice.

PETER: A follower of Jesus, absolutely secure in his faith. In his own sweet way, he is as condescending as Klautus.

JESUS' FOLLOWERS are indicated at several places in the text but they are assigned no lines and the play may be performed without them.

The action of the play takes place in Palestine between the death of John the Baptist and the death of Jesus.

1: *Judas* is to be done in modern dress on a modern set. Pilate's office is corporation sleek, Mary's kitchen anything from cheap chrome to rude wood—I suggest the latter, so it may double as an outdoor café table in the street scenes.

2: The reader should not expect Jesus to be the central character. In my play the Jesus-Mary relationship is an echoing subplot to the Judas-Pilate relationship, which is central.

3: Herod was not killed by the crowds, nor did he kill Herodias. The throne of Judea was vacant at the time and Jesus was expected to take it. Since people persist in thinking that Herod was king, I have disposed of him and his wife to clarify the political situation. Incidentally, Herod did not kill Salome either, except in Wilde's play, to which mine is a sequel.

4: Joseph, in the Gospels, shares Mary's visions of Jesus' divinity. I have deprived him of this insight in order to have conveniently at hand an example of a frightened, ordinary Judean of the day.

5: Pilate and Jesus were never alone. But in spite of being notoriously antireligious, Pilate did try to save Jesus. I have given them a closet scene to explore possible reasons why.

6: Pilate and Judas are not acquainted in the Bible, although there is a medieval legend that Judas was Pilate's page.

7: Klautus and his family are wholly invented.

8: The reader's attention is called to the fact that scenes interlock. That is, the last lines of a given scene are said alternately with those beginning the next.

9: I would prefer the play to be done without intermission. One is, however, indicated in the script.

10: I like intense, precise acting. *Judas* was in part inspired by Salvador Dali's paintings "Illumined Pleasures," "The Font," "The Old Age of William Tell," "Palladio's Corridor of Dramatic Surprise," "The Lugubrious Game," and "Geopoliticus." The reader will not go far wrong to imagine my play in Dali's hard, hot light, nor to picture my characters' faces and bodies being distorted by emotion as the play proceeds, in the manner of the Spaniard's tortured images.

Judas
Robert Patrick

A C T   O N E

S C E N E   O N E

PILATE's *office in the Tower of Antonia in Jerusalem. There is a desk piled high with books, two chairs, a bust of Tiberius on a pillar which also bears a dish of salt for votive offerings. There is a door leading to a hallway and* KLAUTUS's *office, another leading to* PILATE's *private chambers, and a window overlooking* PILATE's *forecourt, with a view as well of the Temple grounds and of all Jerusalem.*

On the wall is a huge and splendid relief of the fasces, the Roman Imperial symbol, a bundle of rods with an axe in the center, tightly bound together.

At rise, PILATE *is at the window, shouting to crowds below.*

PILATE: Barbarians! Barbarians! Barbarians!

KLAUTUS: (*Enters at full attention.*) Sir. Request permission to speak with the Governor, sir. (*Clicks heels.*)

PILATE: Quiet, Klautus, I am attempting to listen to my mob!

KLAUTUS: Sir . . .

PILATE: Now by their screams, if I decipher them correctly, it seems that they are suffering from the delusion that King Herod is here in our towering tower . . .

KLAUTUS: (*With growing nervousness.*) Sir . . .

PILATE: Whereas you know, and I know, that even an idiot like Herod would have the taste . . .

KLAUTUS: Sir . . .

PILATE: Very well, not the taste, but at least the cowardice, to flee Jerusalem after that bloodbath at his palace last night!

KLAUTUS: (*Like an answering machine.*) Sir! Herod of Judea, by proclamation of Tiberius Caesar—Emperor of Rome and of the World—named Native King of Judea, requests an immediate audience with Pontius Pilate, by proclamation of Tiberius Caesar—Emperor of Rome and of the World—named Roman Governor of the conquered province of Judea, sir! (*Clicks heels.*)

5

PILATE: Herod? Here? How did he get through that swarm of his bloodthirsty subjects?

KLAUTUS: (*Imperviously at attention.*) By a secret tunnel his father built into the Tower, sir! (*Clicks heels.*)

PILATE: A secret tunnel. The foundation of all good government. But by your impeccable little schedule, Klautus, isn't is time for young Judas' lesson in statecraft?

KLAUTUS: Young Judas is here also, sir! King Herod insisted his matter was urgent, sir.

BOTH: (*Together.*) And he is the King! (KLAUTUS *clicks his heels.*)

PILATE: (*Flustered and angry.*) Oh, that's the trouble with these puppet potentates. I've told Tiberius that a hundred times. A fine young mind like Judas must wait while I do embassies with imbeciles! Very well, then. Show the monarch in. Is he able to walk by himself?

KLAUTUS: (*Still at attention.*) Just barely, sir! (*Clicks heels, salutes, makes a military turn, steps through the door, and beckons. Instantly* HEROD *rushes in, gibbering, to the altar, where he sprinkles salt before Tiberius's bust frantically.*)

HEROD: Pilate, Pilate, save me, they want to kill me. Look, you know I'm loyal to Rome, look, see, I'm sprinkling salt before the Emperor, see? Hail, Caesar! You know I'm loyal, you know I love Rome, save me, they want to murder me, save me, save me, save me, save me, save me. (*He ends at* PILATE'*s feet.*)

PILATE: (*Disgusted.*) Klautus. Go out there and keep Judas from hearing his anointed King blubber.

KLAUTUS: (*With click of heels.*) Yes sir! (*Exits.*)

HEROD: Pilate, you won't let them ...

PILATE: Hush! Wait until the children can't hear, ninny! (*When* KLAUTUS *is gone.*) All right. Now. What is this idiocy I hear?

HEROD: It's true, Pilate, it's true, it's all true. Forgive me.

PILATE: Forgive? What difference will be made if I forgive? Will that bring back the popular holy man you killed? This, this ... (KLAUTUS *re-enters with a file folder which he spreads before* PILATE. PILATE *consults it as needed.*) ... this John, John, John the ... Baptist? Forgive! Truly you are the superstitious chieftain of a superstitious rabble!

HEROD: (*Who hears only some words.*) Rabble! Yes, yes, yes, they are a rabble. (*At window.*) Rabble! Rabble! Rabble! They want to kill me, make them be still, make them stop screaming!!!

PILATE: (*Takes picture of John from* KLAUTUS.) You've killed a popular prophet. That is the popular reaction.

HEROD: But he preached . . . John preached against the Queen.
PILATE: (*Takes picture of Queen from* KLAUTUS.) That is why he was popular.
HEROD: He said she broke the law.
PILATE: I've read the law. She did.
HEROD: But it was only a stupid native law.
PILATE: You were made king to keep the native laws.
HEROD: But my wife demanded his death, Pilate.
PILATE: But you ordered it, Herod.
HEROD: I know that it was wrong.
PILATE: That does not make it right.
HEROD: But Pilate, you are a man, you will understand. She offered me her daughter. You've seen her daughter, the Princess Salome, you must have seen her. She was arrogant, irresistible . . .
PILATE: (*Takes picture of Salome from* KLAUTUS.) Is that why you had *her* killed after the prophet?
HEROD: No, no, no, it was because I knew I had done wrong. It was to atone for my crime.
PILATE: And what about the crime he was preaching against you for? That ludicrous local law you broke by . . . what was it? (KLAUTUS *hands him relevant headlines.*) By marrying Herodias, your . . . what was the idiot taboo? . . . your brother's wife?
HEROD: I have atoned for that sin, too, mighty Pilate. I had my wife put to death today. (PILATE *looks to* KLAUTUS *in disbelief.* KLAUTUS *nods, hands* PILATE *a last paper, clicks heels, salutes, and exits hastily up center.*)
HEROD: (*To the stunned* PILATE.) Please, please, please, I can't offer you gold, I spent it all on my last coronation, please forgive me, make it all not have happened!
PILATE: Ooooooh, I wish I believed in a God I could blame this on. I know why Rome does not allow us to interfere in local religious matters. For one thing, the mere sight of such ignorant evil must corrupt even the observer. For another, if we leave the followers of any religion alone, they will eventually slaughter each other and Rome will be rid of them! (*Strides to altar, offers salt. Fervently.*) Hail, Caesar!
HEROD: (*Has heard only "Rome," sprinkles salt.*) Rome. Rome. Yes, Rome. You are the hand of Rome. I will be safe if you will only say that Rome forgives me. And I will tear off a hundred of their heads to make them pay for their treason against Rome's designated king!

PILATE: (*With a penetrating stare.*) A hundred or one? Very well, have your magical formula. Your wish has come true. Yes, Herod, of course Rome forgives you. I forgive you. I give you absolution. Rome is merciful. Rome forgives you. Go.

HEROD: (*Sighs.*) Oh, thank you, Pilate. Thank you. You will see. (*Up off his knees.*) A Herod never forgets. I will be good now for as long as I live. (*Exit up center, smirking and preening.*)

PILATE: (*Moving to window with* HEROD'*s picture.*) And I also forgive the crowd of your own people waiting below to tear you into shreds. (*He stands where the people can see, tears* HEROD'*s picture into shreds, showers them on the crowd, and turns "thumbs down," condemning* HEROD. KLAUTUS *enters, clears off the table, organizes the file folder, cleans up the altar.* PILATE *watches the spectacle below, unmoved.*)

KLAUTUS: (*With a polite cough.*) Sir. Are you ready to see young Judas, now?

PILATE: Am I ready, after that hopeless hysteric, for a chance to educate a clean young mind? Yes, Klautus, I am ready. Send him in. Close that window. Send the crowd away. Get someone to hose down the courtyard. We're off schedule. (KLAUTUS *obeys;* PILATE *moves to desk.*)

KLAUTUS: Yes, sir! (*Exit with folder.* PILATE *picks up a notebook, dons glasses.*)

JUDAS: (*Irrupting in, distraught, with briefcase.*) Pilate!

PILATE: (*Super-cool.*) Good to see you, Judas. So sorry you were kept waiting.

JUDAS: Didn't you hear? The people have murdered Herod?

PILATE: Never mind, Judas, he died good.

JUDAS: But they've torn him to pieces in your own courtyard!

PILATE: It's good to see them get together on something.

JUDAS: But Herod was our king! You put him over us as king!

PILATE: Well, then, we must get you another. (JUDAS *is rushing to window.*) Don't touch that window! (JUDAS *freezes;* PILATE *speaks not without kindness.*) Judas, the careers of kings rise and fall like fountains splashing in a philosopher's garden. Now, having mentioned philosophy, tell me—open your notes and tell me—what were we discussing yesterday?

JUDAS: (*Hesitant, but obeying.*) You ... you said that today we would inquire into the relationship between religion and money.

PILATE: (*With gusto.*) Ah, yes, good. Now. Let's see. Let us begin with a hypothetical situation. Let us say, Judas, that you found

Laird Williamson (PILATE) *tearing up the picture of* HEROD *in the* PCPA *production.*

yourself in a jungle, surrounded by ravenous cannibals. What would you do?

JUDAS: I'm only an executive trainee. I don't know.

PILATE: Of course you do. You are an intelligent boy. You would invent God. And quickly, too. You would convince those cannibals that God did not want them to eat you. And if that worked, you might go on, always using the authority of God, and create sweeping social reforms. You might get them to feed their poor, keep their cities clean, treat one another kindly and fairly. You might improve their culture in every way. It would have every surface form of civilization. But! You would still be surrounded by cannibals who believe there is a God. And the first time you failed them, they would eat you. Or if a challenger arose they would choose between eating him and you. And if they encountered another tribe who had a different name for God, they would eat them. A civilization based on a lie can only go so far. Do you see that? Are you listening to me?

JUDAS: (*Who has been gazing at shutters.*) Oh, yes. Yes, sir. I see it. I've seen it just now. I . . . I fail to see its relationship to money. (KLAUTUS *enters with tray of wine and biscuits, places it on desk.*)

PILATE: You may go, Klautus.

KLAUTUS: Yes, sir! (*Clicks heels and exits.*)

PILATE: Come, think now, Judas. In the same situation, you might as easily come up with the idea of money, and pay them not to eat you. And similarly your civilization would thrive until it met one that did not use the same money. Now do you see? (*Wine and biscuits throughout this scene.*)

JUDAS: It's . . . very difficult to talk with you about some things, Pilate. We are taught that our God is . . . God. The only God.

PILATE: You were taught to save your money, too. And now it is worthless unless it is valued in Rome.

JUDAS: Yes, you've said you'll take our God into your temples and give him a Roman name.

PILATE: And he will be popular, I'm sure. Gods of all nations find followings in Rome.

JUDAS: (*Aware he is on dangerous ground.*) And . . .

PILATE: (*Amused.*) And what, Judas?

JUDAS: And are all those gods lies?

PILATE: (*Watchful, pleased.*) That would follow from our initial example, yes.

JUDAS: And all those nations?

PILATE: By extension, yes, that would follow.

JUDAS: And is Rome...

PILATE: Go ahead. Speak your mind, Judas.

JUDAS: (*With a burst of courage.*) Very well. Isn't Rome a lie, then? Isn't Rome a lie, like any other nation? (*Backing down.*) I ask only in the spirit of philosophical inquiry, which you yourself have taught me, Pilate.

PILATE: (*Delighted.*) What a joy is a mind that is not afraid of truth! Yes, Judas, of course, Rome is a lie. It is the last, necessary lie. But it is run by men who know the truth. You are training to be one of those men.

JUDAS: If that is so... If I am to know the truth you speak of, then... how is Rome different from any other nation? Lie? How is it better? How can you give your life, and other lives, to it? It doesn't seem better, only stronger. It doesn't seem to change anything. It didn't stop the killings today.

PILATE: Rome did not do today's killings, Judas. As for its superiority, watch. Klautus!

KLAUTUS: (*Enters much too quickly.*) Yes sir?

PILATE: (*Taken aback, but firm.*) Klautus, issue an edict. From this day the Jews of Jerusalem may no longer execute death sentences, neither by stoning nor decapitation nor crucifixion nor in any other manner.

KLAUTUS: (*Making as if to go.*) Yes sir.

PILATE: Oh, and Klautus...

KLAUTUS: (*Military turn and heel-click.*) Yes sir?

PILATE: Also, from this day, office staff may not eavesdrop on conversations in the governor's office.

KLAUTUS: (*Without reaction.*) Yes sir. Will that be all, sir.

PILATE: It had better be. (KLAUTUS *salutes, clicks heels, and exits.*) There, I've been meaning to do that anyway.

JUDAS: Certainly. I see. But what will you do to anyone who breaks that edict?

PILATE: Do? I don't know. Kill them, probably.

JUDAS: You see? All right... Rome didn't kill John and Herod.

PILATE: Or Salome or Herodias.

JUDAS: Yes, yes, of course I know that, but... oh...

PILATE: Judas, never hesitate. You have my word that you may always speak freely here.

JUDAS: (*With new courage.*) Very well. You say so. All right. Rome kills. Rome has killed millions. Rome got to be Rome by killing.

You got Judea by war and killing.

PILATE: And bribery and conniving with the Herods. Don't forget that.

JUDAS: I'm going too far. I just meant that Rome kills, too.

PILATE: Judas, when Pompey was called to Judea, the fragments of your tribes were killing one another like idealistic jackals. Rome did not start the killing here. Rome has very nearly ended it. Look, you see this symbol every day. (*Indicates fasces.*) Do you know what it means?

JUDAS: It's everywhere. It's the symbol of power.

PILATE: It is the secret of that power. It is called the fasces. The word means "bound together." Each of those rods was once the scepter of one Italian tribe. They warred incessantly until they bound themselves into one irresistible corporate state. Your twelve tribes were once bound together by King David, and then Judea ruled the Mediterranean. But there was a terrible error in its organization: it was bound by belief in religious rigmarole. You've seen today what that brought Judea to: superstitious squabbling and slavery.

JUDAS: (*Indicating Tiberius's bust.*) And are Romans any less super- stitious slaves because you worship a man and call *him* God? Oh, I know, I know: I have that in my notes. (*He flips through notebook to find page. Reads.*) "Julius Caesar saved Rome from tyranny under Pompey. Cassius saved Rome from tyranny under Julius Caesar. Marc Antony—for whom this very fortress tower was named, did you know that, Judas?—saved Rome from tyranny under Cassius. They would have gone on saving Rome from each other until there was no Rome to save. But Octavian, when he saved us from tyranny under Marc Antony, had the sense to declare himself a god. No one, you see, could accuse god of tyranny. Wasn't that clever? And he was able to pass both throne and godhead peaceably on to Tiberius. The result is that for sixty years Rome has existed without the necessity for a major tyran- nectomy!" (*Closes book.*) So . . . no one believes it.

PILATE: (*Who has listened with pleasure.*) The second or third gener- ation usually does.

JUDAS: So. Rome is a lie. Judea is a lie. You're asking me . . . us . . . me to give up one lie to accept another?

PILATE: I am asking mankind to discontinue defining itself as races and religions, classes and clans. Each such definition is a declara- tion of war. I am asking mankind to bind itself together.

JUDAS: Oh, I know you're right. You must be. Rome is the most successful organizing force in the history of mankind. You must be right.

PILATE: (*Thoughtfully.*) Each man must join the tribe. Each tribe must join the nation. Each nation must join Rome. But first each must unite the warring forces within. (*Simply.*) Judas, are your people giving you trouble because you were chosen to be trained for Rome?

JUDAS: My people? Trouble? Oh, no.

PILATE: (*Knowingly.*) No? Then you are unique.

JUDAS: Oh, well, certainly, some of my friends. Not the bright ones. And some old people. But most of my friends envy me. And my parents brag about me. Even our high priest. Do you know our high priest, Caiaphas?

PILATE: Oh, I know Caiaphas quite well. He was here only this morning, to beg me for the loan of his sacred robes for eight days, so your people may celebrate their deliverance from bondage.

JUDAS: (*Aware of the irony.*) Yes. Well. Caiaphas says I'm doing the right thing. He says our religion has survived only by changing with the times. Only . . .

PILATE: Ah, at last an "only." "Only" what, Judas?

JUDAS: Only, I don't see how a religion can change and still have been true. You've told me, I have it in my notes (*Flips notebook.*), here, (*Reads*) that "religion gives form to a civilization." If the religion changes, then mustn't the civilization collapse?

PILATE: Hasn't it? But the collapsible civilizations last the longest. Yours is proof of that. Caiaphas is right, Judas. The fragment of your religion that prevails will be the one that takes on the forms of Rome.

JUDAS: (*Almost worn down.*) Pilate, everything you say is true. It's logical, it's irrefutable, it all makes sense up here in your tower. But there's something left out of it, something you can feel in the streets. I don't know what. But there's something without a name in the blood, in the beating of the heart, that wants, that loves, that needs . . . a family, a nation, a race, a religion, a . . . name. The Rome that you describe has no—how can I say it?—no heart.

PILATE: It has my heart, Judas. It has had it since I was a boy. Give it yours and it will have two hearts. Someday it may—it must—have the hearts of all the world.

JUDAS: But for all that, men still fight you, still fight Rome. Belief
    . . . belief is very strong. Men are willing to die for their beliefs.
PILATE: Men do not die for their beliefs, Judas; they die from
    them. Or if they live and will not abandon belief in the face of
    moral logic, then they live crucified on their own contradictions.
    You will learn, all men will learn, that it doesn't matter what
    people believe, as long as they all believe the same thing. When
    all nations are one, men will see they never needed nations.
    When all monies are one, men will see they never needed
    money. When all gods are one, men must see that they never
    needed gods. (*Heads for altar.*) But to bring that about, each man
    must bind himself to the strongest. I do, when I say, "Hail,
    Caesar." (*He is at the altar, reverently offers salt.*)
JUDAS: (*Sincerely.*) And I when I say, "Hail, Pontius?"
PILATE: (*Interrupts, embarrassed.*) Oh no my boy, no, not that,
    never that. (*Pause.*) Now, think . . . and speak again.
JUDAS: (*Comes to altar, hesitates.*) I was taught to say, "Hail, Judea,"
    "Hail, Jehovah," "Hail, Herod." I no longer say those.
PILATE: And you cannot yet quite bring yourself to say, "Hail,
    Caesar"?
JUDAS: (*Bravely.*) No. No, I cannot.
PILATE: (*With kindly tolerance, leads* JUDAS *away from altar to
    window.*) You have time, Judas. We are at peace in Judea, now.
    (KLAUTUS *enters with a scroll, catches* PILATE's *eye, indicates his
    watch.* PILATE *takes scroll, motions* KLAUTUS *to wait.*) The holy
    man who raised the rabble against the queen who enraged them
    by marrying the king who feared them all, all are dead. (JUDAS
    opens window. PILATE *and* JUDAS *stand looking down.* KLAUTUS
    clears wine paraphernalia.) The symbols of good and evil have
    killed each other. If we could see through the roofs of those mud
    huts, we would see happy families preparing for their ritual
    holiday.

MARY *enters, in shawl, with shopping bag, the area downstage
that will be Joseph's house. The two scenes run concurrently until*
PILATE, JUDAS *and* KLAUTUS *exit.*

MARY: Jesus, John is dead in Jerusalem, awake!
JOSEPH: (*Runs in after* MARY, *in work clothes, stops her.*) Mary,
    what are you doing?

PILATE: Here the war is over. Judea is part of Rome.

MARY: (*Fighting* JOSEPH.) Jesus, awake, awake, they have killed John! (JOSEPH *throws her into a chair.*)

JUDAS: Oh, Pilate, I . . .
PILATE: Yes, Judas, you hope so?

JOSEPH: You'll have the Romans on us.

JUDAS: No, but I hope that I may hope so.

MARY: We *have* the Romans on us!

PILATE: (*Delighted.*) Honest Judas! Come, (*Brandishes scroll.*) let me show you the plans that have come from Rome!

JOSEPH: Mary, be still.
MARY: Jesus, awake!

PILATE: (*Moving to door with* JUDAS.) The plans for the pantheon!

JOSEPH: Let the boy rest!

PILATE: (*Exiting with* JUDAS.) The temple of all gods! (KLAUTUS *follows with wine tray.*)

SCENE TWO

JOSEPH's *home. The kitchen. Table, three chairs. Door to street, through which* MARY *and* JOSEPH *have entered. Door to garden. Door to* JESUS' *room.*

MARY: (*Rising.*) Rest! With the blood of our murdered king screaming for revenge?
JOSEPH: (*Making her sit.*) Herod wasn't our rightful king, Mary, you said so yourself.
MARY: (*Pounds table in impotent rage.*) Not Herod, John! John! John!
JOSEPH: (*Closes* JESUS' *door, seats himself.*) John was our relative, Mary, this house will be watched. We need time to think.

MARY: We have had centuries to think. What is there to think with, Roman logic? Did I bear a child to see him a Roman slave?

JOSEPH: We're not slaves, Mary. The Romans treat us better than anybody ever did. John was crazy.

MARY: They murder us in the streets!

JOSEPH: Only if we rise up against them.

MARY: Do we dare lie down before them to see?

JOSEPH: Mary, look, have you thought of this? Ninety years ago we were murdering each other over whether Hyrcanus or Aristobulus should be king or high priest or neither or both or whatever.

MARY: They were Hasmonean pretenders!

JOSEPH: And we had to call the Romans in to settle it!

MARY: And they brought a reign of bloodshed and terror!

JOSEPH: Which is what we had before, Mary, don't you see?

MARY: You talk like that Roman tool Caiaphas! A high priest for Roman slaves!

JOSEPH: And which of our priests are better? They fight on the street corners until they drive a man crazy! And the Romans let them, so what are you yelling about?

MARY: They look down from their tower gloating when we fight! They want us to fight!

JOSEPH: So stop it!

MARY: And you know who we should fight. They take our lives, they take our way of life! They defile our temples, they break our Sabbath.

JOSEPH: Mary, they rule seven countries in a row with seven different Sabbaths! If they didn't break some of them, they'd never get anywhere!

MARY: This from a son of the holy house of David!

JOSEPH: Everyone's from the house of David, Mary; it's that long ago. Your family says it's from the house of David, too.

MARY: Yes!

JOSEPH: It doesn't mean anything. Our kings haven't been from the house of David for a long, long time!

MARY: And now the alien, usurping line is ended.

JOSEPH: Well, isn't that what you want?

MARY: I want what you would want if you were not a sleeping dog! I want what we have a right to. Our leader, our law, our language, our land God gave to us!

JOSEPH: That we took from the tribes of Canaanites, you mean!

MARY: God gave us victory over the Canaanites!

JOSEPH: And he gave the Egyptians, and the Babylonians, and the Persians and the Greeks victory over us, and he gave the Romans victory over them! Have you thought of that? Have you thought of this? If you're right, why doesn't the boy agree with you? Hm? He's smarter than you; he's smarter than anyone. Why does he fight you, huh? Have you thought about that?

MARY: Because he has been waiting for the proper time, and that time is now, with John's followers gathering in Jerusalem!

JOSEPH: John was crazy, Mary! Now, with our relative beheaded, now's the time for us to go on our knees to the Romans for forgiveness!

MARY: You dare say this to me on the very eve of Passover!

JOSEPH: If it is the eve of Passover. Nobody knows! They can't agree what time of day to start the Sabbath or how sacrifices should be made or any of the old things.

MARY: And so if a prophet comes, a prophet with divine insight, to renew and clarify it all, to unite us against them . . .

JOSEPH: Look, have you thought of this? You're always quoting scriptures at me, okay, have you thought? If all the people that were left after the flood were Noah and his family, like the scripture says, then aren't everybody alive now Jews? Huh? Have you thought of that?

MARY: What are you saying to me?

JOSEPH: Yes, I thought that would stop even you.

MARY: Stop me? Do you know what you've said? Does he speak even through you? You are saying to me that his mission will be to all mankind? His power over all? Oh!

JOSEPH: Oh, God, Mary, whose mission? Whose power?

MARY: Our prophet, Joseph, our *king* . . .

JOSEPH: (*Claps his hand over her mouth.*) Mary, if there's one thing our priests agree on it's that God has spoken to us for the last time. I don't care how many lunatics chased him, most of our people didn't recognize John as a prophet, much less as . . . what you said.

MARY: Not John! Not John! No! Jesus! Jesus! Jesus!

JOSEPH: Don't start that!

MARY: Look what he has done already! Half our people took Passover at Mount Gerazim. Who showed them their error, who taught them that Jerusalem was our one true holy city?

JOSEPH: (*Head in hands.*) Our son, dear Lord, our son.

MARY: Yes, and this year all the tribes assemble there, some say three million.

JOSEPH: That's all the Romans need, three million. They'll smell rebellion.

MARY: Already thousands follow him.

JOSEPH: Thousands followed John, Mary.

MARY: Yes! And they will be added to the followers of Jesus! It is in our blood. John, our cousin—my cousin—Elizabeth's child, roused our nation against an adulteress who had defiled our holy house. Of course he failed. He died. But he has cleansed that house. Perhaps some other woman is meant to fill that house, to restore our greatness, to be Queen Mother in Judea!

JOSEPH: Mary, you make me crazy when you talk like this. Can't you hear what you're saying?

MARY: Then do not make me say it! I have other things to say! (*Heads for* JESUS' *door.*) Jesus, awake! (JOSEPH *grabs her, holds her back. The door opens and* JESUS *enters.*)

JESUS: I am awake, mother.

JOSEPH: (*Releases* MARY.) See if you can do anything with her, son. You're the one that taught her to read.

JESUS: (*As* MARY *enfolds him.*) Yes, father, rest, rest.

MARY: Have you heard what happened?

JESUS: John is dead. Herod is dead. The people tore him to pieces in Pilate's own courtyard.

MARY: (*To* JOSEPH.) You see?

JOSEPH: They're screaming it in the streets, he's heard.

JESUS: John was alone, he sent his people to follow me, I knew it would happen.

JOSEPH: Everyone knew it would happen.

MARY: But not like my son.

JESUS: Many people said it.

MARY: But you knew, you saw, you foresaw . . .

JOSEPH: (*Pleading.*) Mary . . .

JESUS: Mother, if I did, then must what I feel now must happen, happen? If everything I feel must happen must happen, then is there no hope?

MARY: (*Correcting him.*) There is no *doubt!*

JESUS: Mother, I don't know how much you know. I read you the scriptures, I tell you all that I can bear to tell, but you never seem to listen.

David Williams (JESUS), *Richard Rieble* (JOSEPH), *and Kathy Brady* (MARY) *in the PCPA production.*

MARY: I listen. I know. You know I know. (*Touches amulet around his neck.*) Look, you wear this symbol every day. Have you forgotten what it means?

JESUS: Have you ever *known* what it means?

MARY: (*Ignoring him.*) It is the serpent Moses set up in the desert to draw the tribes together. The serpent on the sticks.

JESUS: On the cross, mother.

MARY: The tribes had been scattered by a plague of serpents.

JESUS: And now they are scattered by a plague of prophets! Who must be raised before the tribes now, mother?

MARY: One who has within him things that are within no other man!

JOSEPH: Mary, you'll make yourself sick this way!

JESUS: Mother . . .

MARY: No other man, do you hear me, Jesus?

JESUS: Mother . . .

MARY: No man, Jesus, no man at all.

JOSEPH: Mary, stop.

MARY: No man, Jesus, do you hear me, what I say?

JESUS: I wonder if you know what you say.

MARY: No man . . .

JESUS: Mother! If a man . . .

MARY: No man!

JESUS: Yes, a man! Only a man! If a man must take all the things that we have been taught, and somehow, in the world we live in, make them work for everyone . . .

MARY: He must first be placed very high, yes!

JOSEPH: Mary . . .

JESUS: That is not what I was going to say.

MARY: It was, it was, you needn't hide it from me. Speak in parables elsewhere, but you know you may always speak freely here. Mayn't I know the thought? Shouldn't I know the thought? Didn't I . . .

JESUS: (*Jumping at her supposed error.*) Yes, mother, didn't you what? Plant the thought there?

MARY: (*Avoiding his eyes. Cool.*) Foresee it all. Was I not told? Was I not allowed to see?

JESUS: Told, mother? Who told you?

MARY: (*Coiled pause.*) Why, you did, Jesus. Who told you?

JESUS: When did I tell you? What did I tell you?

JOSEPH: Mary, leave the boy alone, you can see he's not well.

MARY: He has been too much alone. The people call him. They call him to Jerusalem. (*To* JESUS.) Remember how we took you to Jerusalem? How you felt the call? Remember how we gave you to the temple?

JESUS: The temple, the temple. You sacrificed two doves. I felt something then.

MARY: You baffled the wise men in the temple for three days!

JESUS: Three days was all it took to baffle them. Our leaders! They knew no answers! None! And now I have traveled to every end of Judea, I have read racks of books, I have talked with the evil and the innocent and the insane and no one could give me an answer.

MARY: You are the answer.

JOSEPH: (*Warning.*) Mary . . .

MARY: John said that you were the one!

JESUS: Mother . . .

JOSEPH: Mary, not John, please.

MARY: The one that we all should follow, the one to bring our people together . . .

JOSEPH: Don't bring our people together, God, they'll fight!

JESUS: (*To* JOSEPH.) And they do, you see? They do follow me.

MARY: Of course they do. They see.

JESUS: So many . . . thousands . . .

MARY: Now millions.

JESUS: (*Conjuring the scene.*) You don't have any idea what it is like to see thousands of faces turned toward you, like blind flowers aching for the sun, to stand above them and hear their voices . . .

MARY: Yes, yes?

JESUS: Or to hear the silence . . . when you pause to take a breath. The silence that means they want you, they need you, they need more . . .

MARY: Oh, wondrous, wondrous!

JESUS: (*His reverie breaks.*) Is it? How much do you think I can give? How much do you think they need? Mother, how much, how much do you know?

MARY: I know what they all know, what they all see, I know that you are sent to take the very highest place.

JOSEPH: Stop!

MARY: What?

JOSEPH: If anyone overhears what you were about to say . . .

MARY: What? What are we about to say?

JOSEPH: No, don't. Leave me out of this. I don't want to know. I don't want to see . . .

MARY: You see, Jesus? Your father sees it too.

JOSEPH: I don't!

MARY: Oh, yes, he does. Your father sees, Jesus. Your father knows.

JOSEPH: I don't. I don't.

MARY: I never said *you* did.

JESUS: (*Very carefully.*) My father is not in the position that you seem to me to be referring to, and I could not take that position if he were not before me in that place.

MARY: (*Trying to draw him out'*) Your father is not in that place. That place is for you.

JESUS: And my father?

MARY: (*"Two can play at this game."*) The father of one in that place cannot be lower than the place you speak of, can he? Or his son would not have so high a place as that place you know we *are* speaking of.

JESUS: Then the father of such a man would be . . .

MARY: Higher!

JESUS: Only the Romans are higher!

MARY: Higher!

JESUS: There is no man higher!

MARY: (*With the smile of an adoring girl.*) There is no man higher.

JESUS: (*After a pause.*) I am mad.

MARY: (*Turning away, politely normal.*) Why would you say that?

JESUS: John was mad.

MARY: John was, too?

JESUS: And his mother, too, I think.

MARY: Well, then, why stop there? Was not Herod mad, and Salome? And Herodias? And the people that followed the one and condemned the other and have slain the other two? Not mad, any and all of those? All, all not mad?

JESUS: Yes! And you, who would send me out as Elizabeth sent John and Herodias sent Salome, we are all mad!

MARY: Then who is not, your . . . father here, who thinks he can read our minds?

JOSEPH: I don't. I can't. I never said that. I don't know what the two of you are talking about. I won't be dragged into this . . . craziness.

MARY: So! We are confirmed that we are mad. Then we will be for all the rest of our lives a family of mad people? Crazy people? Living in a mud hut, crazed, twisted, uncertain, forever asking?

JESUS: Asking?

MARY: Forever asking!

JESUS: And never answering?

MARY: (*Challenging.*) Ask! Ask straight out and it shall be answered!

JESUS: (*Backing down.*) I can't. You know I can't. Or if you don't know that I can't, and why I can't, then it is impossible all the more.

MARY: Then be mad! Whatever these ideas are in your head, you cannot blame me for them. I don't even know what they are. I have merely been trying to follow your poor mad rambling thoughts, as I have always done, ever since you came up with these ideas, which have always haunted you, which you have felt ever since you were a little child, yes! long before you can remember, you have had these ideas, they have always been a part of you.

JESUS: You sang these thoughts to me!

MARY: (*Wooing him.*) I wove into my songs the thoughts you spoke when first you learned to speak, the thoughts you seemed so certain of, so clear about, though of course I did not understand them, do not understand them even now, I got them from you, they came from your lips while you were still in the cradle, such thoughts! they seemed to come from . . . from you. They seemed then to give you peace, certainty, comfort, calm, those things you seem so to lack now, certainty, comfort, peace, purpose, calm . . .

JESUS: (*To* JOSEPH.) Father, is this true?

JOSEPH: I don't know, son. Don't ask me. I never heard.

MARY: He could not hear, he was not there, I was there, I alone, I know, I am the only one who knows, the only one who heard how soon, how strong, how clearly these thoughts came to one whom others saw as nothing but the son of a carpenter, *a carpenter and the son of a carpenter!*

JOSEPH: Mary, spare me that. At least, spare me that. (*He rises to leave.* JESUS *stops him.*)

JESUS: Father. No. Don't. Don't be . . . unhappy. Please. We should love everyone. We should love everyone.

MARY: Is that so? Do you know that? How do you know?

JESUS: (*Draws* MARY *to him as well.*) Whether they are our father, or our mother, or not, we should love everyone. I cannot endure their pain, God.

MARY: Pain?

JESUS: (*Looking up, speaking.*) I can endure my pain, God, I can suffer it forever, but do not torture me with their pain. Show me the way to take their pain from them. I want only for them to be happy. I cannot be happy unless they are happy, unless everyone is . . . happy. And all that I see around me, in this house, those streets, in the mobs beseeching me, is pain!

JOSEPH: (*Pulls away in fear and embarrassment.*) Son, don't . . .

MARY: (*Leaves* JESUS, *sits at table, croons.*) Who can make all men happy?

JESUS: (*Strangely still.*) God can.

MARY: (*Croons.*) God will send a prophet to make all men happy.

JESUS: It is written so.

MARY: (*A secret smile.*) Is it? Is it written, too?

JESUS: Too?

JOSEPH: Mary, don't start. Son, don't let her do that to you.

MARY: (*Croons.*) And Herod tried to slay the prophet.

JESUS: (*Moving slowly to* MARY.) He slew all the male children under two years old.

MARY: (*Croons.*) Who was under two years old?

JESUS: I was. But you took me away.

MARY: (*Croons.*) How could a mother know to take her son away?

JESUS: Many mothers may have done so.

MARY: (*Croons.*) Many mothers may have done so.

JESUS: We wouldn't know. They would all lie.

MARY: (*Croons.*) But how did I know to take you away?

JESUS: Someone told you.

MARY: (*Croons.*) Is there any other way I might have known?

JESUS: There is, one other way . . .

MARY: (*Croons.*) Is there an old prophecy that I might have read?

JESUS: There are, that you might have, that could be taken as a warning . . .

MARY: (*Croons.*) Then that must be.

JESUS: (*Kneels at her feet.*) Yes. Yes, it must.

MARY: (*Croons.*) But Herod slew the king of Israel. If he had been born. If he was among those children.

JESUS: People say that it is, that it was John.

MARY: (*Croons.*) People say that it was John. I have heard people say that.

JESUS: Mother. We are speaking of horrible things. Why do you smile?

MARY: (*With serene calm.*) At my thoughts, Jesus. My own private thoughts. Which you cannot know. If people cannot know one another's thoughts.

JESUS: Mother, people said that John was that prophet. And Herod slew John.

MARY: (*Intellectual, puzzling it out.*) Herod slew him that people said to be king of the Jews?

JESUS: Many people still say it.

MARY: Many people think that Herod slew the rightful king of the Jews?

JESUS: Yes. Herod is dead. John is dead. Let them rest.

MARY: So, the world is safe for the Romans?

JESUS: Yes.

MARY: The Romans think they are safe?

JESUS: (*Stands, turns away.*) They are.

MARY: (*With unleashed passion.*) Jesus, listen! The Romans think they are safe!

JESUS: (*With finality.*) And they are. They are.

MARY: (*Defeated, raging.*) Oh, yes! For Herod, who tried once to kill the king of the Jews, and failed, has tried again and succeeded. And the people have killed Herod! And now the Romans will kill the people!

JESUS: No, now the people are happy!

MARY: While they live!

JESUS: They live!

MARY: While the Romans say, "Live!"

JESUS: There is always someone to say, "Live!" and someone to say "Die!"

MARY: Unless something higher says, "Stop killing!"

JESUS: (*Ultimatum.*) There is only one power higher!

MARY: (*"Check!"*) And does it not say anything of the sort? To anyone? I had hoped someday it might. Who can tell us? Who can tell us to stop fighting, if that is what is right? I knew a little boy who loved peace . . .

JESUS: And who has known none of it.

MARY: He lives in a land where it is unknown.

JESUS: He lives in a house where it is unknown.

MARY: In a house, in a land, in a world, in a universe where peace is unknown? Perhaps. Perhaps not. Who can tell us? Who will take it upon himself to tell us? Who can say if there is any hope of peace in life? Or after life? Who will tell us? Who knows? (*She exits to the garden.*)

JOSEPH: (*Looking after her.*) Jesus. Try not to be so hard on your mother. She was always like this, she has spells, she's working up into one now. I know she gives you a hard time, but . . .

JESUS: (*Sits at table, head in hands.*) She? She is no more than a wound Israel bleeds through. She says aloud what the faces say, what your face says.

JOSEPH: Now, son, don't say that. I'm happy the way things are.

JESUS: But she will not, or she cannot, say it all. And I can no longer tell whether I would rather be confirmed and be certain or whether I would rather never know and have the voices that clang in my brain be only some mad raving song of hers!

JOSEPH: Son, don't say this to me, I can't help you.

JESUS: And I am afraid even to ask her what I would die to know, because she would only have to look at me and say, "Son, you are mad; that thought is madness," and I would be lost. She holds my mind in her hands like a cat's cradle and waves it in front of me, as if she could weave it straight, or fling it away . . .

JOSEPH: Son, why tell me these things? I don't understand.

JESUS: Or tangle it, God, tangle it so that not even she could straighten it again. Oh, God in heaven if there is a way out of this tangle, tell me . . .

JOSEPH: Son, don't do that. Does he? Does he really . . . speak to you?

JESUS: (*Not without humor.*) How would I know if he did? Do you see? How would I know if it was his voice, or hers, or my own? Not speech, God, but a sign. If I am to do what seems to be laid on me, give me a sign to show I know the way!

MARY: (*Re-enters, dazed, as if blinded.*) Revelation! Son! It is a miracle! I understand! I understand what you have been trying to tell me! A lifetime has come clear! Everything illuminated! The way is straight! A million things you told me come together. My son . . . (JOSEPH *attempts to help her, but she shoves him away. She will accept only* JESUS' *help. They sink to their knees, face to face.*) You feel that you are the savior, prophesied of old to lead our people! Back to the old ways, the unity of the tribes! All the old prophecies! All the old things, they seem to untangle and lay themselves in a line! Jesus, my son, can it be that I am blessed, that you are he, that I was chosen to bring man life? (JESUS *stands so that she is in effect kneeling to him. He cannot break her handhold on his own.*) Are you indeed the son of God, God made man, God come in human form to save us? Suddenly it seemed so to me. I admit it. I confess it! Am I alone in that thought? Am I insane? Oh, help me! Help me from this pain! Can I never be sure of anything again?

JOSEPH: Mary!

JESUS: Mother!

MARY: (*Pulling him down to her.*) You must answer me. You must help me. Only you can. Tell me, *is* a person insane who thinks these thoughts?

PILATE *enters upstage in his office, idle and bored. He picks up binoculars and wanders to the window.*

JESUS: (*Helping* MARY *rise.*) Oh, come with me. Come with me and tell me. One by one. Step by step. Tell me all you saw.

PILATE *begins to scan the view from his window, not looking toward the family scene.*

JESUS: (*Leads* MARY *off into his room.*) No, no, no, you are not, you need never, ever, be alone again. (*They exit.*)

KLAUTUS: (*Enters office, holding pouch of mail.*) Ahem. Sir, would you care to go over the mail from Rome now?

JOSEPH: Oh, God! If you can hear us, if you care . . .

PILATE: (*Turning to observe* KLAUTUS.) Hmmmmm. On the whole no, Klautus, I would not.

JOSEPH: I don't ask you to tell me. I don't ask you to show me.

PILATE: I would much prefer to stand at my window, (*Turns again to window.*) overlooking Jerusalem.

JOSEPH: But, everything has passed out of my hands. I only want you to save us. Save him. Save her.

> PILATE: Oh, I love this tower, Klautus!

JOSEPH: Save all of us. (JOSEPH *exits.*)

SCENE THREE

PILATE*'s office. Day.*

PILATE: One can see patterns so prettily from here. The raveled city reweaves itself out of its recent disorder. Pilgrims and merchants feed through the gates into the gently geometric precincts of a crowded holiday town. Oooh, I really should have been an orchestral conductor! (*Looks to right.*) Look, over there one can see Herod's palace, so unfortunately empty now, and still. Tsk-tsk-tsk-tsk. (*Leans far out, looks right.*) And there at the end of the way stands Golgotha, for the moment mercifully free of its familiar forest of crosses. (*Looks straight out.*) And down there in the gaping mouth of the theatre, Andromache bewails the fact that her little son must die so the Greeks can survive to sow the seeds of Rome!

KLAUTUS: (*Unimpressed.*) Yes sir. And here is the diplomatic mail.

PILATE: (*Ignoring* KLAUTUS.) And spread out at my very feet is the swarming but ordered temple, where some decorative snag has occurred in the festival fabric of ritual. Hm. Some poet, no doubt, selling the always marketable tale of past glorifications and power to the people. But! doing it in his proper, traditional place. Indeed, indeed, I dearly love a tower. (*Turns, sees* KLAUTUS, *smiles.*) Why, hello, Klautus, I didn't see you come in. (*Ignoring the proffered mail.*) Isn't it time for Judas?

KLAUTUS: Judas is not here, sir. The mail is.

PILATE: He's never late. I hope he isn't ill!

KLAUTUS: (*Slyly, matching* PILATE*'s cool.*) I should imagine, sir, he would be one of the crowd at the temple attending the new prophet. I'll put the mail here if I may, sir. (*Lays mail on* PILATE*'s books, would leave.*)

PILATE: Prophet? Are we with prophets again, already?

KLAUTUS: (*Politely remaining.*) Yes sir.

PILATE: Is that what that excitement is down there?

KLAUTUS: Yes sir. The young man has expelled the money-changers from the temple, sir. You know, the ones who exchange Roman coins for the sacred coins with which the pilgrims may buy sacrificial animals?

PILATE: Oh, he's in trouble. They don't like interference with their temple. When I came to Jerusalem, I put up statues of Caesar all around the temple grounds. Four hundred Jews stormed it because of some taboo against "graven images."

KLAUTUS: Yes sir. Maybe that's why they don't like our coins, sir.

PILATE: I ordered them to disperse or I would have their heads cut off!

KLAUTUS: Yes sir. You showed strength, sir.

PILATE: Yes. So did they. They bared four hundred necks to the blade. I took down the statues, sent them home, and started studying their religion.

KLAUTUS: (*Moving to window.*) Well, sir, this one is not in trouble. They're moving to him like . . . like . . .

PILATE: (*Supplying a phrase.*) Pond scum?

KLAUTUS: Yes sir. Look, they're turning their backs on their priests.

PILATE: (*Joining* KLAUTUS *at window.*) Yes, there's old Caiaphas in his borrowed robes.

KLAUTUS: And they're gathering around the prophet like . . . like . . .

PILATE: Flies around a camel's rectum?

KLAUTUS: Exactly, sir.

PILATE: That's unkind, Klautus.

KLAUTUS: But, sir, they should by rights be stoning him.

PILATE: Why, I forbade them to.

KLAUTUS: Well, I know, sir, but if they had any spirit. He's said he'd tear their temple down.

PILATE: He *didn't?*

KLAUTUS: (*Unaware he is being toyed with.*) I was there, sir; I heard him. Then he said he'd rebuild it in three days!

PILATE: Oh, why is he doing this at Passover? Any other time I'd be happily home in Caesarea regulating the impost tax on pomegranates. Hmmm. Why *is* he doing this at Passover? Did you say three days?

KLAUTUS: Yes sir.

PILATE: Three days. (*Moving to his books.*) That echoes something in one of their earlier prophets. (*At desk, sees mail.*) What is this on my books?

KLAUTUS: (*Joining him at desk.*) The mail from Rome, sir.

PILATE: Why is it on my books?

KLAUTUS: Well, sir, Judas *is* missing, and we *did* formerly utilize this time to discuss your correspondence.

PILATE: I'm sure Judas is only late, Klautus. And my studies of this province are at least as important as Rome's senatorial conspiracies, your father excepted, of course.

KLAUTUS: Of course, sir.

PILATE: (*Handing mail to* KLAUTUS.) So do something else with your diplomatic pouch! (*Flipping pages.*) Here, see? Three days. Yes, here it is. A symbol of rebirth in the book of... ah... Jonah. There, you see? Hmmm. Did this young man by any chance enter Jerusalem on a white colt?

KLAUTUS: (*Too surprised to say "sir."*) Why, yes. To a great crowd. Troops were called out!

PILATE: (*Holding two books, delighted.*) I knew those verses connected! (*Lays books down. In a high good humor.*) We needn't fear for the temple's integrity, Klautus; he's ony exploiting old prophecies as John did. When you become governor of a province, Klautus, study the local religion, no matter how bewildering. Not only will it afford you much amusement, but it will clarify much that is otherwise baffling in the behavior of the... recently Roman. But I should not have thought our Judas was one to loiter on street corners listening to bugaboo stories... even if you are.

KLAUTUS: Possibly not, sir.

PILATE: You do not share my fondness for Judas, do you, Klautus?

KLAUTUS: Sir, it is not my place to...

PILATE: Oh, Klautus, talk to me as you used to. This tower is a Roman ship marooned among your pond scum. Talk to me like a Roman.

KLAUTUS: Well, sir, since you ask me, no, I am not fond of these people.

PILATE: They have not had your advantages, Klautus, your faith in our holy mission, your awareness of the emperor's divinity, your certainty that our forebears were suckled by a giant she-wolf: your rational Roman upbringing. Surely you can sympathize with those less fortunate?

KLAUTUS: Oh, yes sir. I even think I understand why they follow these prophets. The young Jews are looking for leadership, rebelling against the old order.

PILATE: Of course they are. The old order promised them the world, and it hasn't delivered. But it is not the lie they are rebelling against; it is the truth. Most rebels are only closet conformists, trying to make true the lies they were told in their cribs.

KLAUTUS: I can see that. That's very interesting, sir.

PILATE: Yes, but it is not very relevant. Klautus, what do you think is the hardest task of a ruler?

KLAUTUS: You told me last week, sir: the education of the masses.

PILATE: Wrong. The masses are easy to educate. They believe each week whatever they are told. No, it is the intelligent who are hard to educate.

KLAUTUS: This is another one of your paradoxes, sir.

PILATE: The intelligent educate themselves so easily, so early. Their complex minds create sustentacula to support the contra-indications of their cultures. That is the difficult task, to locate the bright minds before they are twisted and hardened under that burden.

KLAUTUS: I'm not sure I understand, sir.

PILATE: No, that's what I was saying. Look, you think I lavish too much time on Judas?

KLAUTUS: (*Hurt.*) You are the governor, sir, and if you choose to . . .

PILATE: That won't do, Klautus! You must understand! A young man is a sensitive thing, he needs approval and appreciation, a great deal of appreciation and approval.

KLAUTUS: (*With meaning.*) I'm aware of *that,* sir.

PILATE: (*Missing it.*) You may think that a young man's main concerns are sex and sport, food and sleep, but you are wrong, Klautus, wrong! A young man's main concern is morality. Young men want to be good, to make good. That is why they are obsessed with authority, with testing it, *protesting* it, they *want* an authority, someone to tell them the rules of the game of goodness. They want virtue's prize, whether it is an athlete's wreath, a merchant's millions, a panjandrum's power, or a hero's grave! So! The best ones will be, not the least, but the *most* loyal to their past and people, most faithful to their first faith. They must be helped and eased out of their familial, fanatical, philosophical, patriotic bind!

KLAUTUS: Yes sir. But what you're really talking about is traitors, sir.

PILATE: Who will Romans be but traitors to all the other nations?
This very fortress tower was named for that traitor Marc Antony!

KLAUTUS: (*Shocked.*) This tower, sir?

PILATE: Put your feet down, Klautus. He was not a traitor when it
was named. He was winning. Traitor! Traitor is a touchy word.
You know very well that I was born Spanish and that I personally
opened my city's gates to the Romans.

KLAUTUS: Yes sir! Of course, sir!

PILATE: Treason in the cause of Rome cannot be treason, can it?

KLAUTUS: No, sir, but . . .

PILATE: But?

KLAUTUS: (*Escapes to window.*) These people aren't even loyal to
their own faith, sir. Look at how they're behaving down there! I
mean, to have a religion that irrational to start with . . .

PILATE: "Damned if they do . . ."

KLAUTUS: And then not even to follow it!

PILATE: "And damned if they don't." And what if I were to tell you,
Klautus, that far from being irrational, they have been brilliant?

KLAUTUS: I don't see how you can say that, sir. They don't even
have anything of their own. Everything they have is from one of
the countries where they've been slaves!

PILATE: No material culture, no.

KLAUTUS: And they've always *been* somebody's slaves, you can't
deny that.

PILATE: (*Starting a game.*) And yet every power that has ruled the
world has been only a period in their history. How do you think
they have maintained themselves as a nation throughout their
defeats and dispersals?

KLAUTUS: I suppose, sir, that no one would mix with them.

PILATE: Not only that! They have made themselves a nation of the
mind, something we are just learning to do. (*At desk.*) In these
wormy books there is organizational genius. Their God, to begin
with, is their God alone. They make no effort to proselytize
others to his worship.

KLAUTUS: Then it's no religion at all.

PILATE: Ah, but it makes them feel very special. What's more, he
has no face, no name, dwells in no idol or altar, so he is with each
of them always, everywhere, cannot be captured.

KLAUTUS: They probably just couldn't defend a temple.

PILATE: Plus! They have a tradition of nonconformity . . .

KLAUTUS: Now, that's a paradox!

PILATE: (*Ignoring him.*) Not official oracles as we have, but a *tradition* of inspired prophets. So that a Jew of any rank who has a necessary idea can get attention by claiming to speak with God's voice!

KLAUTUS: But any charlatan could fool them that way, sir.

PILATE: So you are listening. Good. But all of this is child's play compared to their political masterstroke.

KLAUTUS: Political! What politics can they make out of a God that's always defeated by other gods!

PILATE: That's it! Somewhere among their captivities, when they themselves were grumbling that their God was overpowered, some masterful mind among them came up with the final seal on their covenant with their God. They declared that he was the only, the one and only God!

KLAUTUS: Sir, that's simple treason!

PILATE: You see how original? Their hardships were not the work of superior deities, but proof of the power of their—the—God!

KLAUTUS: (*Near breaking point of exasperation.*) But why would they keep on worshiping a God that does nothing but enslave them?

PILATE: Because they see their enslavement as punishment for some huge ancient offense, and if they can keep faith with God until their term of punishment is done, he will forgive them and lead them out of their bondage to their destiny!

KLAUTUS: (*Almost screaming.*) What destiny?

PILATE: Oh the usual I suppose: world power.

KLAUTUS: (*Screaming.*) But what was their offense?

PILATE: (*Punch line.*) That's what they're always wrangling about!

KLAUTUS: (*Regaining his dignity.*) Sir. I understand what you're saying. Insofar as it can be understood. But it's not a religion. It's not politics. It's madness. No sane man would countenance it for a minute. It's a mass of . . . contradictions?

PILATE: (*Interested.*) Near enough.

KLAUTUS: And I don't believe they believe in it themselves!

PILATE: Klautus! You're right. You're brilliant. You've seen right to the core of it. We will win! They are historically weary of prophet after prophet, of promises and purges. Look, now, (*He drags* KLAUTUS *to window.*) they're following this new one off to the mountains to be blamed and blessed again. And Caiaphas stands fuming in his forecourt, ready to blast them all when they return. You're right. They're ready to cast off their nameless,

faceless God. He would have to come down among them himself
to regain them. We're just in time. They are ready for a god in
human form. (*Turns to bust of Tiberius.*) Hail, Caesar! (PILATE
sprinkles salt gaily. KLAUTUS, *not quite sure what he has done right,
but delighted, joins him and repeats ceremony.*)

KLAUTUS: Hail, Caesar!

PILATE: My boy, you'll go far. Shall we convince Tiberius to
declare himself the only god?

KLAUTUS: Sir, to take even an idea from these . . .

PILATE: Squabbling mudwasps?

KLAUTUS: (*"You're not catching me again."*) If you say so, sir.

PILATE: Control your mind, Klautus; think of it as a conquered
idea. Ah, this is what makes rulership exciting. Come, as a
reward, I'll neglect my studies; we'll look at your almighty mail!

KLAUTUS: (*They move to desk.*) Yes sir! (*Clicks heels.*) The letter that
seemed to me to be the most important I took the liberty of
placing atop the stack, sir. It is an Imperial edict (*He goes automatically to attention.*) bearing Caesar's personal seal. It em-
powers you to appoint a new king of Judea from among the
available candidates, if any. Or to let the kingship lapse forever if
you choose. *That's* exciting!

PILATE: (*Unaware how he is deflating* KLAUTUS.) Oh, bore! Kings
again? Why? Now that all kings are one, can't men see that they
never needed (*Catches himself about to commit treason in front of*
KLAUTUS.) Oh, if only there were some promising local like
Judas who didn't spend his time doubting and debating. Have
they grown up, or do they need a king. What do you think,
Klautus?

KLAUTUS: Well . . . I think, sir, they have the Emperor in Rome!

PILATE: Yes, but have they the strength to bear some part of the
burden of Rome?

KLAUTUS: (*Shocked.*) Burden, sir?

PETER *has entered the street below, with a big bag of pamphlets to
distribute. He looks for a suitable place, and sits center.*

PILATE: (*Wryly.*) Burden, sir. Oh, come, let us go look at the
answerable mail. (*To window.*)

KLAUTUS: Yessir. (*He gathers mail.*)

> PETER *sees someone coming and hops up, pamphlets held in left hand, right hand out to shake hands.*

PILATE: (*Musing at window.*) Have they?

> JUDAS: (*Entering with briefcase, checking watch.*) Who is this man? (*He stops and looks back.*)

PILATE: Have they?

> JUDAS: Who is this man?

PILATE: (*On his way out door.*) Do they need a king? (KLAUTUS *follows* PILATE *out.*)

SCENE FOUR

A street in Jerusalem. PETER *is onstage, ready to pass out pamphlets from a shoulder-bag on which is stenciled* JESUS' *emblem, the snake on the cross, and the words* "Follow Him."

JUDAS: (*Very disturbed, to himself.*) Who is this man? Who is this man?

PETER: (*Stops* JUDAS *with handshake and pamphlet.*) I am called Peter.

JUDAS: (*Flustered, digging for coin for pamphlet.*) Oh. No. Pardon me. I am called Judas. I am pleased to meet you. (*He has to set down briefcase to shake hands, give coin.*) I meant . . . that man that speaks on the mountain, what is *his* name, where does he come from, not you.

PETER: He is from Nazareth, in Galilee.

JUDAS: (*Stopped by this.*) You know him?

PETER: I follow him.

JUDAS: (*Trying to be polite.*) You see, when I was coming past here, just now, I was not really talking to you, or to anyone . . .

PETER: (*He has done this before.*) I know. I stand here, just beyond the crowd, and I wait, for such as you, who need, perhaps, to talk with someone.

JUDAS: Aha. Then he is always as he was today.

PETER: I did not hear him speak today. I cannot always hear his words from here. I do not need to hear him so often anymore. His words since first I met him have gone on in me. It is enough for me to see that he goes on.

JUDAS: Yes, he is . . . a most effective speaker.

PETER: (*With a smile.*) Is he? What does he say effectively?

JUDAS: Well, I cannot quote his exact words.

PETER: I think you can. I think you will. I think you are another one of us.

JUDAS: I am a Jew, and a Roman, if that is what you mean.

PETER: Oh, that and more! Judas, what did he say today?

JUDAS: Well, he said . . . (*Looks off where* JESUS *stands.*) It's strange. I should remember. There was no murmuring in the crowd at all. I heard every word. But I was looking at the crowd, the way they all stood looking up to him, listening, and smiling, and it seemed so right. They stopped breathing. They stopped quarreling. And I was the only one watching them instead of him. That's typical of me. I had to leave. I had an appointment. I'm late. He is . . . a most effective speaker. (*Starts to go.*)

PETER: Judas. Dear brother. (*Kisses him.*)

JUDAS: (*Jumping away.*) Please. That is not a custom in my particular . . .

PETER: (*Joyfully.*) In your particular dark miserable loneliness. Oh, Judas, I shall pray for you tonight.

JUDAS: With him? (*Slaps pamphlet in* PETER'*s hand.*) I no longer pray. (*Starts off.*)

PETER: You will.

JUDAS: I am a Roman now.

PETER: Oh, we are all Romans. What has that to do with . . .

JUDAS: (*Uncertain why he is staying.*) Everything! (*Embarrassed.*) I don't understand what you're talking about. Nothing. Everything. (*Starts off.*) Everything.

PETER: (*Not moving.*) Judas, turn back.

JUDAS: (*Stops, wheels.*) What does that mean? How did you mean that?

PETER: Judas, do not see everything as hidden. Nothing is hidden.

JUDAS: (*Trying to regain dignity.*) I did not say anything was . . . hidden.

PETER: Everything seems hidden at first, but we are here . . .

JUDAS: We? You mean you and I? Or you are all here for me?

PETER: (*Claps his hands in delight.*) Judas, Judas.

JUDAS: If you want to be effective, you must not speak in riddles. That is why I left my faith, riddles and mysteries. That is the way of the sophists and pharisees.

PETER: It is not I who speak riddles, Judas. Nothing is confusing. (*Moves toward* JUDAS.)

JUDAS: It is. Stay away from me.

PETER: (*Stops.*) Oh, Judas, why fight the love you feel inside?

JUDAS: (*Laughs.*) It is not love that I feel inside. You are one of them, one of that . . . superstitious rabble.

PETER: I follow him. Is that superstition? He moved you. Are you rabble?

JUDAS: Stay where you are.

PETER: I know what you're going through, Judas.

JUDAS: You don't.

PETER: Then tell me, Judas; tell me your thoughts. You want to, you know.

JUDAS: Speak my mind freely? That is what people say when they want to know your innermost thoughts.

PETER: Oh, I wish I could.

JUDAS: You are so cool. So smooth. Have you done this before?

PETER: Done what?

JUDAS: (*Advancing.*) Tried to entrap loyal Roman citizens in this . . . web? (*Strikes pamphlets from* PETER's *hand.*)

PETER: (*Humbly retrieving pamphlets.*) What web? I don't know what you mean, Judas.

JUDAS: (*Ashamed, sits.*) Oh, yes, you do.

PETER: First you are angry because I say I know your thoughts, now you are angry because I say I don't. I don't understand you, Judas. (*With the smile.*) What are you fighting? I told you, be a Roman.

JUDAS: What, and spy on them for you?

PETER: Oh, or spy on us for the Romans, if you are a spy. What do we do that anyone else does not do? What do any men do that others do not do?

JUDAS: Men do horrible things. They make war, and they kill.

PETER: (*Moving to him.*) Oh, Judas, would you make war on me? Would you kill me? I hope not.

JUDAS: (*Moving to watch* JESUS.) That was what it was . . .

PETER: What?

JUDAS: That was all it was. He spoke as if he would not, and could not.

PETER: Ah.

JUDAS: I cannot remember what he said. I hope I will. I never realized before that all men seemed always to be . . . threatening me, to be telling me what to do, to shape me into something. But he spoke—as if only to unwind my fears. He spoke, as if he could do—would do—no harm.

PETER: (*Entranced, forgetting his mission for a moment.*) Oh, I wish that I could speak like that.

JUDAS: (*Turning to him.*) Why? To lure me into what?

PETER: Not to *lure* you into anything.

JUDAS: What is this? Suddenly even someone like you seems threatening. *Did* other men seem threatening before? Or is it only because I have seen him?

PETER: (*Feeling a failure.*) Maybe. After him, certainly.

JUDAS: And is he merely one of you that has learned the trick? What is he trying to draw me into?

PETER: Only yourself, Judas, believe me. Nothing more.

JUDAS: Myself? But it is you I am afraid of.

PETER: (*Indicating his general mildness, laughing.*) Me?

JUDAS: Yes, yes, I know, I see. But there is something more that you are not telling me.

PETER: Nothing that I know.

JUDAS: (*Not without humor.*) Yes. Perhaps that is why you are not telling me.

PETER: (*Back on familiar ground.*) Or, Judas, perhaps it is something within yourself, something you have not put into words. (*Extends pamphlet.*)

JUDAS: (*Almost takes pamphlet.*) No. Their way is better.

PETER: Whose way?

JUDAS: The Romans.

PETER: (*Almost angry for a moment.*) We were not talking about their way of doing anything. (*Recovers himself.*) Why do you speak so much of the Romans?

JUDAS: Perhaps because they are . . . trying to lure me into Rome.

PETER: Ah! Are they?

JUDAS: You see? You are prying!

PETER: I am merely trying to understand you. Do you do things that cannot be known?

JUDAS: (*With self-mockery.*) No, no, I do nothing wrong. I am a good boy. I am a good student. Everyone assures me. Everyone forgives me. I'm late for an appointment now, but I am sure I'll be told it's all right.

PETER: (*Puzzled.*) I will speak with you another time.

JUDAS: Oh, you're just . . . you street people, you don't understand anything that's happening to you. You try to live your lives by images out of stories. Look, you're born into the world, see? And everything in it already belongs to someone else. And they tell you you can work and earn some of it for yourself, but the truth is they can take it all away any time they want to pass a new law. And worse than that, they tell you you have choices to make, that you're responsible for your life, that decision is the mark of a man. But the fact is that the world is already split up into sides, and the only choice you really have—if you even have that—is which side to join. And the worst thing is that any side you join, you have to give up everything the other sides have to offer. No, that's not the worst. The really worst is that whatever side you do join, you're automatically betraying all the other sides. No, worse, you're born on a side, you're born a traitor, even before you're born, you're a traitor to most of the people in the world.

PETER: (*Stunned by* JUDAS*'s pain.*) Poor Judas.

JUDAS: But they don't mean it to be that way, that's the worst thing. They mean well, they're all just thinking of your good, unless it's all just pretended so they can get more people on their side. But why would they do that, lie to get you on their side? Why would they want stupid people on their side? Unless they're all of them after something different than they say? What are they after? The worst thing is that you can't trust any of them really to tell you the truth because they've got so much at stake. Everything. They've got everything, so they've got everything at stake. The worst thing of all is that unless you become one of them, you can never really know anything. And then it may be too late. You—people like you—you don't know what you're dealing with. What am I saying? What are you doing to me?

PETER: Nothing, Judas, I'm only listening to you.

JUDAS: It's as if even you were trying to teach me something.

PETER: (*Wanting to help.*) Oh, I wish that I had something to teach you.

JUDAS: (*Looking off toward tower.*) At least I know that he is definitely trying to teach me something.

PETER: (*Looking opposite way, at* JESUS.) Oh, yes. He is the great teacher, he can help you.

JUDAS: No, not him. I meant someone else.

PETER: It must be someone very fine if you can still think of him after hearing Jesus.

JUDAS: Stop! I don't want to know another name! Say something else.

PETER: What should I say?

JUDAS: Anything. Say "Hail Caesar."

PETER: (*Shrugs.*) Hail, Caesar.

JUDAS: You don't mean that . . .

PETER: Well, it's only words.

JUDAS: It's not. It's more. It doesn't mean to be, it doesn't even have to be. But words carry so much weight . . .

PETER: I only said them because you asked me to.

JUDAS: If I don't know his name, then there is nothing tied to what I have just gone through. I had a glimpse of something, and I can remember it. And . . . I had a glimpse of what they are all trying to do.

PETER: Who?

JUDAS: (*Would say "everyone" but knows* PETER *would not understand.*) The Romans.

PETER: (*Thinking he understands.*) Oh, yes, indeed, they are, but it is . . .

JUDAS: (*Incredibly alone.*) If there were no words . . .

PETER: (*A familiar and comfortable thought.*) Yes.

JUDAS: (*Thinking he might communicate.*) Then . . .

PETER: (*Thinking he's on the beam.*) Maybe.

JUDAS: (*Desperate.*) Maybe *what?*

PETER: (*To him it's obvious. Laughs, would kiss* JUDAS.) Oh, my dear Judas.

JUDAS: (*Recoiling, gathering briefcase.*) I don't want to talk to you anymore.

PETER: (*Puzzled.*) I'm sorry.

JUDAS: I don't want to know you or see you again.

PETER: It will be my loss.

JUDAS: I don't want to know your name. I have forgotten it. And his. And everything we have said.

PETER: Judas, you can't. Believe me.

JUDAS: I don't want to . . . infect you with the sickness and doubt I have found within myself.

PETER: Are you sick?

JUDAS: I want to be. I'm going to be. I'm late. I don't care. I'm tired. I'm tired of their temples.

> *Lights up on* PILATE'*s office, late at night, books piled on desk, no one present.*

JUDAS: I'm tired of their towers. Where's a tavern? Is there a bar around here? I want to get drunk! I want to be as sick as I feel! (*He takes money from his pocket, grabs pamphlets from* PETER, throws money on ground, throws pamphlets on ground, reneges, takes one pamphlet, grabs his briefcase, and flees, fast.*)

PETER: Oh, Lord, I have been guilty of conceit. I thought I understood this young man's heart. I thought he only felt the same self-doubts and unworthiness I felt before you changed my name and claimed my heart.

> JUDAS: (*Offstage of office.*) Hail Caesar! (*Pounding on door.*)

PETER: (*Kneeling to gather money and pamphlets.*) But he is more troubled, he is beaten and pursued by demons, I hae failed!

> KLAUTUS: (*Off of office.*) Judas! Shut up that racket!
> JUDAS: (*Off.*) Hail Klautus! I want to see Pilate! Hail Pilate! I want to see him right now!

PETER: (*Brightening.*) But if they are so troubled as all that, then how much more eager even than I will they not be to find your glowing peace!

> KLAUTUS: (*Off.*) What are you doing here at this time of night?
> JUDAS: (*Off.*) I want to see Pilate. I told you. I want to see him right now!

PETER: (*Rising.*) He will come to you! They will all come to you!

> KLAUTUS: (*Off.*) What are you up to? What time is it? Look what time it is! You're drunk!
> JUDAS: (*Off.*) I want to see Pilate, Klautus! Go get him? That's what you do, isn't it? Go tell him!

PETER: There now. Now I am not even sorry that I made him ill! (*Exits to* JESUS.*)

SCENE FIVE

PILATE*'s office. Night. Faint light. Books on table.*

KLAUTUS: (*Off.*) You're crazy! Get out of here and come back
tomorrow when you're supposed to! Where were you today?

JUDAS: (*Off.*) Never mind where I was. I'm here now. I'm late for
today or I'm early for tomorrow, but I'm here!

KLAUTUS: (*Off.*) All right. All right. All right. If you really want to
see what you're getting into. Okay. I'll get him. And then, oh
boy, will you get it! (KLAUTUS *enters in shirtsleeves, sees books.
Shouts off to* JUDAS.) He was up until all hours reading. Wait until
you see what he does to you. Are you gonna catch hell! (KLAU-
TUS *exits into* PILATE*'s private chambers.*) Sir? Sir. Wake up, sir.

PILATE: (*Off.*) Huh? Klautus? What time is it?

KLAUTUS: (*Off.*) It's after midnight, sir. Judas is here to see you.
Shall I send him away?

PILATE: (*Off.*) Huh? Judas? Is here? To see me?

KLAUTUS: (*Off.*) Yes sir. Here's your robe, sir.

PILATE: (*Enters in pajamas, followed by* KLAUTUS, *who helps him
with robe. Trying to grasp situation.*) Judas is here to see me?

KLAUTUS: Yes sir.

PILATE: At this hour?

KLAUTUS: He said it was urgent, sir. Insisted it was urgent.

PILATE: And you let him in?

KLAUTUS: Well, sir, you are so fond of him I thought I'd show
him in.

PILATE: I will decide who is shown in around here, Klautus!

KLAUTUS: (*Delighted.*) Yessir! I'll gladly throw him out. (*Starts off.*)

PILATE: I will decide who's thrown out around here, Klautus!
Show him in!

KLAUTUS: Yes, sir!

PILATE: Wait! (KLAUTUS *pauses.*) Judas is a most intelligent and
inquiring young man, an asset to the Empire, and he is welcome
here at any time. Remember that!

KLAUTUS: Yes sir.

PILATE: Good. (KLAUTUS *stands awaiting orders.*) Now go! (*Quickly.*) And don't you click those heels at me again!

KLAUTUS: Yes sir! (*He opens the door and* JUDAS, *clothes disordered,
hair tousled, drunk, breaks in.*)

JUDAS: Pilate . . .

PILATE: (*Entirely for* KLAUTUS*'s benefit.*) Judas, how very good of
you!

Mark Harelik (JUDAS) *and Laird Williamson* (PILATE) *before the fasces in the* PCPA *production.*

JUDAS: I know it's late. (*To* KLAUTUS.) I know it's late!

PILATE: It's no such thing. It's late when a person is tired or sleepy. I am neither (*Noticing* JUDAS's *disarray for the first time.*) and you do not look *sleepy.* (*To* KLAUTUS.) Klautus, coffee. (KLAUTUS *exits.*)

JUDAS: I wouldn't have come . . .

PILATE: No, I'm glad.

JUDAS: But I like to come here. It's clean here. Do you know how clean it is here?

PILATE: (*Vaguely regarding room.*) Yes, it is clean. (*Stupidly.*) It's cold, but it's clean.

JUDAS: I am not clean. I'm troubled.

PILATE: Why, you do me great honor to come to me at such a time. I hope I can deserve it.

JUDAS: How could you deserve it?

PILATE: By being able to help you.

JUDAS: I don't think anyone can help me.

PILATE: Ah. Well, then, what is it you would have of me?

JUDAS: Pilate, I am . . . deeply troubled. (KLAUTUS *enters with coffee, sets it on desk. He has donned his jacket offstage. He stands at attention.*)

PILATE: I see that you are. Be assured that I am indeed desirous of helping you, and that if I can do no more than merely listen to your troubles, then I will be glad to do only that. (JUDAS *does not respond.*) You may go, Klautus.

KLAUTUS: Yes sir. (*He exits, military-style.*)

JUDAS: How do you know that merely listening might help me?

PILATE: Well . . . (*He pours coffee. Coffee-business throughout the scene.*)

JUDAS: Because that is what I felt.

PILATE: I see.

JUDAS: That merely to say it might help.

PILATE: Say what, Judas?

JUDAS: No, but tell me, how did you know that, that merely to say it might help, might be what I wanted?

PILATE: That is often the way with troubles, Judas, especially young men's troubles.

JUDAS: Then other men are like this?

PILATE: We are all alike in some ways, Judas.

JUDAS: Yes, that is what I felt, but that is what is so frightening.

PILATE: My dear . . . I was going to call you "son," but I have not that right. Judas . . . Iscariot is it not?

JUDAS: Yes. You remember my name.

PILATE: Judas, you are very dear to me.

JUDAS: Why?

PILATE: Because you are bright, and eager, and what Rome needs.

JUDAS: Yes, yes, but . . .

PILATE: And I like you, too, of course I do.

JUDAS: How did you know that that was what I was wondering?

PILATE: I talk of Rome so much one might think I had no human life.

JUDAS: Rome is not human?

PILATE: It is not human, it is a name for . . .

JUDAS: No, please, that is not an important point. I should go. (*He tries to straighten his clothing.*)

JUDAS: Judas, a man trained to think in tens of thousands must sometimes seem a little cold by habit. Perhaps I should more consciously make friends with you.

JUDAS: (*Sharply.*) For the good of Rome?

PILATE: (*Only slightly scenting something.*) It will be good for Rome.

JUDAS: And if it were not?

PILATE: I cannot think how it might not be.

JUDAS: (*Sags.*) I can't either.

PILATE: (*Amused, off guard.*) My child . . .

JUDAS: It is only that my mind is open to all possibilities tonight.

PILATE: Yes, yes.

JUDAS: That bar—the line of men in that bar—all smiling. Smiling. Why do men smile and smile as if to reassure someone? Are they afraid? I am afraid. (*Almost getting it.*) If other men are as afraid of me as I am of them, then I am afraid of their fear of me, and my fear of their fear of . . . (*Loses it.*)

PILATE: (*Tactfully.*) Judas, perhaps it is time you had a wife.

JUDAS: Yes, perhaps it is.

PILATE: It is something of a . . . deep and philosophical nature that is troubling you?

JUDAS: (*Horselaugh.*) I think so, yes.

PILATE: We do not live in our minds alone.

JUDAS: Where? What else?

PILATE: There are our bodies.

JUDAS: Yes, I have seen your plans for the body of Rome!

PILATE: No, no, I mean our own bodies. There are pleasures and pains of the body.

JUDAS: But there is more, there is more, you all speak as if there is more. I say that because of the tone of your voice!

PILATE: I keep forgetting how very serious you are. Yes, of course, there is . . . the spirit.

JUDAS: The spirit.

PILATE: That thing with which we make gods and art.

JUDAS: Gods.

PILATE: Yes, we have spoken often of gods.

JUDAS: Not often enough.

PILATE: I seem to remember not long ago . . .

JUDAS: I do not criticize you.

PILATE: I do not think you do, no.

JUDAS: Am I forbidden to?

PILATE: Judas, no. Have I forbidden you any question? Have I been at fault in teaching you?

JUDAS: How can I know? Only you know what it is that you are teaching me.

PILATE: I know what I know that I wish to share with you.

JUDAS: Then is there nothing in all that you have taught me that should have spared me *this?* I am in torment and I don't even have the words to tell you so.

PILATE: You need not be ashamed of pain, Judas. There is nothing weak or wrong in feeling pain.

JUDAS: This pain is wrong. I know it. No one could be meant to feel this pain. I do not want to be torn between loyalties.

PILATE: Judas, are you so torn?

JUDAS: Shall I be tried before the prelates of Rome?

PILATE: Judas, do not make me your tormentor!

JUDAS: No, no, no, I know it isn't you. Forgive me. No. You think asking for forgiveness savage.

PILATE: Not in the sense you mean. Of course, I forgive you. You are in pain. I am your friend. I want to help your pain, to help you from your pain.

JUDAS: I am in pain because I do not know what is right to do. I cannot endure that pain, because it is with me always, every-where, cannot be conquered. I do not think anyone can endure that pain. I feel myself altering, dissolving into nothing but pain. Am I to be a creature made of pain? What good can that do *anyone?*

PILATE: Judas, believe me, I know what it is that you are suffering.

JUDAS: Then why aren't you suffering? Oh, you are; *I'm* torment-ing you.

PILATE: Judas, listen to me; you wish to do good.

JUDAS: If I know what it is.

PILATE: What you are feeling—and be proud you feel it—is the moral pain!

JUDAS: Then others feel it, everyone lives with this?

PILATE: No, most men settle for the first easy answer, the first system that will bind the single stars together into constellations for them and give what is nameless a name. But all philosophers feel it.

JUDAS: (*Pulling pamphlet from his pocket.*) And all holy men?

PILATE: (*Seeing the situation in a new light.*) If I understand you.

JUDAS: (*Throws pamphlet down.*) If we understand them.

PILATE: Judas, if I understand you, this is too important to discuss tonight. You need to sleep. Your mind and body are overwrought. (*He heads for door to call* KLAUTUS.)

JUDAS: And my spirit?

PILATE: (*Weary, waiting.*) Certainly your spirit.

JUDAS: That which makes gods and art?

PILATE: Exactly.

JUDAS: And kingdoms?

PILATE: (*With a certain pride.*) I think it plays a part.

JUDAS: And is the spirit that which cries out to know, to have its mind know what to tell its body to do?

PILATE: Yes, just that.

JUDAS: And if the spirit is ill?

PILATE: Then the mind is likely to feel ill, and the body.

JUDAS: And if the mind is ill?

PILATE: Then the spirit may be tried, and the body weakened.

JUDAS: And if the body is ill?

PILATE: Then, of course, the mind and spirit can be damaged.

JUDAS: (*In great pain.*) What am I trying to say?

PILATE: (*With great compassion.*) Only that you do not know what to do.

JUDAS: Only!

PILATE: All men go through it, Judas.

JUDAS: When they come to Rome?

PILATE: When they come to any moment of decision.

JUDAS: And what moment of decision am I at?

PILATE: Only you know!

JUDAS: But can you see? That is what I need someone to tell me!
(JUDAS *and* PILATE *stand helplessly gazing at one another.* JUDAS

breaks and flees the room. PILATE *would follow, but* KLAUTUS *pops in immediately. He begins clearing coffee.* PILATE *wheels from door, scoops up pamphlet, glares at it.*)

PILATE: Klautus, you wolf's cub . . . ! (*Regains some control.*) Tomorrow. Tomorrow I want you to tell me whatever you can learn about this new prophet. (KLAUTUS *brightens.*) Is he speaking sedition against Rome? Is he recommending violent action against the established order? Does he criticize rulers openly?

JESUS' *followers are starting to gather below.*

PILATE: Where does he come from? Who are his followers? How do they meet and what do they do and say? And think and feel and want? How many are they? Are we never to be rid of them? (*Recovers himself.*) And tell me what time Judas Iscariot goes to them, and what passes between him and them.

KLAUTUS: (*Quite pleased.*) Yes sir. Sir?

PILATE: What, Klautus?

KLAUTUS: And is he still to be admitted to you at all hours? (*He beams, expecting a "no."*)

PILATE: What? Oh, yes, certainly. As he chooses. The doors must kept open. He may come or not, as he chooses. (*He is selecting books from desk and starting off to his private chambers.*)

PETER: (*Entering below, carrying* MARY's *luggage.*) All men are brothers! (*He is hawking pamphlets, gathering the followers.*)

PILATE: As he chooses.

PETER: (*Hawking.*) God is our father in Heaven!

KLAUTUS: (*Clicks heels.*) Yes sir!

PETER: (*Hawking.*) The kingdom of heaven is at hand!

PILATE: (*Exiting grandly with books to his chambers, in a burst of rage.*) Why will young men disturb the rest of Rome? (PILATE *exits.* KLAUTUS *stands the briefest second looking after him, then exits to his office with coffee things.*)

END OF ACT ONE

ACT TWO

SCENE ONE

As at end of ACT ONE. PETER, *carrying* MARY's *luggage, is center among followers.* MARY *enters behind and comes directly to him, interrupting his hawking of pamphlets.*

MARY: (*Eyes aglow.*) All men should be brothers, you say?

PETER: (*Sets down her luggage, circulates.*) Yes, yes.

MARY: (*Follows him.*) Under one father?

PETER: (*Quite irritated, trying to be polite.*) Yes, yes.

MARY: The Kingdom is at hand?

PETER: That's right.

MARY: All these things he has said openly? To everyone?

PETER: Many times, many times. (*He is trying to attend to followers instead of to* MARY. *He distributes leaflets.*)

MARY: (*Trying to draw him out.*) And what does he mean? These things he says, what do they mean to *you?* What does he seem to you to be *trying* to say?

PETER: (*Both answering her and hawking pamphlets.*) Trying to say? I don't know what you mean! I've told you what he has said: (*Waving pamphlets.*) All men are brothers! We must love one another! The Kingdom of Heaven is at hand!

MARY: Ah!

PETER: I have told you his commandments, and they are beautiful. (*Hawking.*) Love one another as you love yourselves. Do unto others what you would have them do unto you!

MARY: But the old commandments, "Honor thy father and thy mother," he has said that?

PETER: He says his new commandments supersede them, but, yes, he has said that.

MARY: And has he *told* you of his father?

PETER: His father on earth and his father in heaven, yes.

MARY: And what does that seem to *mean* to you, his "father in heaven"?

PETER: Why, God, of course; God ... (*Hawking.*) God is our father in heaven!

MARY: But does that not seem to you to ... have a *special* meaning?

PETER: Why, no, he speaks very simply. (*Sudden thought.*) Do you mean that *I* am missing something?

MARY: (*A little worried.*) No, no. I wondered how far he had gone
with you.

PETER: (*Beaming.*) Oh, if his words are not clear to you, I am sure
he will be glad to explain them. He always is. (*Puzzled.*) But
surely *you* know his message. You must have always known.

MARY: (*Contemplating him.*) I just thought, some of you seem
closer to him than the others.

PETER: (*Fighting conceit.*) We stay beside him and we take care of
him. We don't let it mean anything to us. (*He is distracted to give a
pamphlet to* KLAUTUS, *who has entered in scruffy streetwear, or his
idea of same.* KLAUTUS *takes the pamphlet gingerly and lingers in*
PETER's *and* MARY's *vicinity to eavesdrop.*)

MARY: (*Genuinely thinking she's caught his drift.*) Aha! You mean
that he belongs to everyone!

PETER: (*Aghast. Righteous.*) I do not think anyone belongs to anyone. I think all slaves should be made free.

MARY: (*As* KLAUTUS *registers hearing* PETER.) Some people, do,
though, belong to mankind.

PETER: (*Sincerely.*) That would be the most horrible slavery I could
imagine.

MARY: (*Catching sight of something offstage.*) Hush, here he comes.
Don't let them know what we've been saying.

PETER: But I'm sure he wouldn't mind anything we've said.

MARY: There are things you obviously do not understand. Jesus!
(JESUS *enters with* JUDAS *and followers.* KLAUTUS *conceals himself.*)
Jesus! I saw you on the mountain! In'the multitude! I saw you
speak!

JESUS: (*Blessing followers.*) Mother! Mother! So much has happened, so much has changed. I am glad. I am. Glad that you have
come. (*Embraces* MARY.)

MARY: (*Clinging to him.*) Oh, I had to, no matter how dangerous!
I had to be here when you tell them!

JESUS: But it is not dangerous, mother, not dangerous anymore.
(*During the ensuing lines, the followers attend the scene, seating
themselves when* MARY, JESUS, JUDAS, *and* PETER *do. One girl gives*
JESUS *a dazzling robe from a package, a robe bearing, conspicuously,
the serpent on the cross.* JESUS *thanks and kisses her and displays the
robe on himself, all during lines.*)

JUDAS: Is this your mother?

JESUS: My mother, Mary. Mother, this is Judas, newly come to us.

MARY: (*Barely nodding to* JUDAS.) There are so many, aren't there?

Thousands and thousands.

JUDAS: I am not, really, newly come to them.

PETER: (*To* JUDAS.) You mean you were always with us.

JUDAS: No, I meant that I am not really with you. I am glad to know you and to learn from you, but I have other commitments.

JESUS: Judas, we feel that you are one of us. You will always be welcome among us.

JUDAS: (*Indicating the crowd with joy.*) But . . . everyone is welcome with you, it seems.

JESUS: (*Only a little condescending.*) And so are you.

JUDAS: (*Hopefully.*) You mean, you extend citizenship in your kingdom to everyone?

JESUS: Yes, if you would state it so.

MARY: (*He has said the secret word.*) Kingdom!

JESUS: (*To all.*) The kingdom of God is open to all who will enter it.

MARY: (*To* JUDAS, *since* JESUS *is elsewhere.*) All who will recognize it.

JUDAS: (*A little confused by Mary's gloss.*) There are things I still don't understand.

PETER: Jesus, your mother too has many questions for you.

MARY: (*To* JESUS.) No, no, I was merely questioning your followers. I was curious to see how much you have told them. I understand. You know I understand. You are gathering your forces. I understand.

JUDAS: There are questions I would like to ask. Sometime. When you *have* time.

JESUS: (*Going to* JUDAS.) Judas, what is our time on earth for, but for each other? Let us sit here now and talk. (*Comes to* MARY.) Uh . . . Peter, take my mother with you and find her a nice place to stay. (PETER *would gladly comply.*)

MARY: (*Seating herself.*) Oh, I must be here to see you begin.

JESUS: As you will. (*Pause, staring at her. Decision.*) Yes. Yes, that will be good. (*Smiles, seats himself.*) Judas?

JUDAS: (*Embarrassed at the center of attention.*) To start with, it seems you seldom speak unless you are questioned.

JESUS: That is true.

JUDAS: As if you wish only to help people, not to . . . preach to them.

MARY: Oh, he can tell you anything, anything.

JUDAS: Yes, it does seem you have an answer. Whatever anyone asks, you have an answer for.

JESUS: I share what I know.

JUDAS: But, what if no one asks the proper questions?

JUDAS: But, Judas, what would be the proper questions?

MARY: (*To* JESUS.) You mean that each man must find them in his own dissatisfaction with the world.

JUDAS: I meant that, if someone came to you in trouble, and needed your help even to understand what was troubling him— could you help him?

MARY: Of course, he could.

JESUS: (*A little piqued at* MARY.) I could try.

MARY: Because he knows.

JESUS: (*Correcting.*) Because I want to infuse everyone with the happiness and peace that I have found within myself.

JUDAS: I am troubled.

JESUS: I see that you are.

JUDAS: Am I . . . a part of this kingdom of heaven?

MARY: You are, of course, if you will swear loyalty to it.

JESUS: (*Without looking at* MARY.) The kingdom of heaven is within. We are all part of it.

JUDAS: But that seems to bring you such peace.

JESUS: That is the kingdom of heaven—peace.

JUDAS: Not war?

MARY: Not unless we are forced.

JESUS: (*First spark of distress.*) No, not war. What has war to do with peace?.

JUDAS: Is . . . is Pilate a part of this kingdom of heaven?

JESUS: Of course.

MARY: What?

JESUS: (*This ought to do it for everyone.*) We are all, without exception, part of the kingdom of heaven—which is only peace— which is within us.

JUDAS: I am not at peace.

MARY: (*Unable to believe her ears.*) Perhaps you have not understood.

JUDAS: I feel torn, torn between loyalties.

MARY: (*To* JESUS.) That is the problem, surely.

JESUS: No. It is no problem, there are no divisions, we are all one. What loyalties, Judas?

JUDAS: Loyalties to you and to . . . to Caesar.

MARY: Ah-ha!

JESUS: (*To* JUDAS.) There is no conflict there.

MARY: Oh!

JESUS: My kingdom is not of this earth.

MARY: Your kingdom. What is your kingdom?

JESUS: The kingdom of God.

MARY: The kingdom of God is *your* kingdom?

JESUS: It is the kingdom of all.

MARY: That is not what you said.

JESUS: Mother, it is long now since we talked. Let us go together later and have a conversation.

MARY: I cannot take you from the people who need you. See how they need you.

JESUS: Mother. There may be much that you do not understand.

MARY: I do not think so. Have you not said, "Honor thy father and thy mother"?

JESUS: (*Weary.*) It has been said, many times.

MARY: Am I not your mother?

JESUS: Have I not honored you?

MARY: And is not God . . . our father?

JESUS: (*Hoping she will understand.*) The father of everyone, yes, yes.

MARY: *Your* father?

JESUS: (*It's hopeless.*) Yes.

MARY: And does Pilate honor our heavenly father?

JESUS: In his way, I think.

MARY: (*Deliberately going public.*) And Caesar? Looting our people, crushing us under the Roman yoke? (*Some of the crowd leave at this dangerous talk.*)

JESUS: You do not understand Caesar.

MARY: Then speak to us of him. Tell us of Caesar.

JESUS: (*To the bystanders.*) I have nothing to do with Caesar.

MARY: No, for you wander free, you do not pay the taxes or heed the laws.

JESUS: (*To the crowd.*) Pay the taxes, then, heed the laws. Render unto Caesar what is Caesar's. I have nothing to do with these matters. My father's kingdom is beyond taxation and laws.

MARY: Are you not the son of the kingdom of heaven?

JESUS: We are all.

MARY: Then should you not claim his kingdom?

JESUS: All of us. It belongs to all of us.

MARY: The kingdom of God? Which god? Of Zeus? Of Capitoline Jupiter? Of the heathen gods they let men play on their stage right here in our holy city? The heathen gods they crowd into their temples? (*More of crowd leaves.* KLAUTUS *ducks behind cover.*)

JESUS: There must be one God.

MARY: Yes.

JUDAS: Yes, there must!

MARY: They say that you have defiled our temple, flinging men you called "disbelievers" out. Will you hesitate—*why* do you hesitate—to defile theirs?

JESUS: (*To both crowd and* MARY.) I found myself following out old scriptures. I entered Jerusalem between walls of smiling people, like a calf going down a chute! Smiling faces lined my way to the temple and there I found a scene set out for me, and like a doll among dolls in the plays you hate, mother, I stood and shouted lines from broken books! They clutched their cages of doves and fled, and all the faces smiled, waiting for me to act out the next scene along the way. And among them one fat face smiled in a secret way, one face that understood, that knew the scene at the end of that way and still could *smile!* And I knew that way was wrong, mother, that way is wrong, those men were worshiping in their way, I had no right to come in and tell them I knew more of God than they, I was no better than the factionalists squabbling in the streets, no better than the fat face of smiling Caiaphas! We have no right to break God up into one more little piece. There must be one nation!

MARY: Yes!

JESUS: There must be one money!

MARY AND JUDAS: Yes!

JESUS: And there must be, forever, one annealing God!

MARY, PETER, JUDAS: Yes! Yes!

MARY: Oh, there is! And he is Caesar!

JESUS: No!

JUDAS: No?

MARY: Then who is he?

JUDAS: Yes, yes.

JESUS: Do not ask, mother, you cannot understand.

MARY: I have asked, (*Points to* JUDAS.) he has asked, the world is asking.

PETER: Jesus?

JESUS: Yes, Peter?

PETER: Can I help you, Lord?

MARY: Hear that? "Lord."

JUDAS: (*To* PETER.) Why do you call him "Lord"?

PETER: What else should I call him?

MARY: (*To* JESUS.) There are prophecies, you know the prophecies, you have fulfilled so many of them, prophecies lined up one behind the other, all, all of them insisting there shall come a savior to our peole, a Lord over us, a King—I say it! King of the Jews.

JESUS: Then perhaps there shall.

PETER: (*To* JESUS.) Many people say that you are he, Lord; you should know that.

JUDAS: (*To* PETER.) They said that John was that prophet, that king.

MARY: (*To* JUDAS.) John himself said that he was not.

JUDAS: (*To* MARY.) His death may have been a terrible mistake.

MARY: (*Confident, staring at* JESUS.) No, his death emptied the royal house of Judea.

PETER: (*To* MARY.) That was a tragedy.

JUDAS: (*To* PETER.) No, it may have been good. Now there is only the royal house of Rome.

MARY: (*Never taking her eyes off* JESUS.) No. There is still the vacant throne of Judea.

JESUS: (*To* MARY.) There are prophecies lined up beyond the prophecies you know, they are dark and secret and twisted and only wise men know them. You have not read them as I have or tried to lay them straight. You do not know the way these prophecies twine, what they clutch at their center!

MARY: I do. I do.

JESUS: Then what?

MARY: You have forbidden me to say it.

JESUS: I am begging you to say it, to see if you do know.

MARY: (*Almost afraid.*) All right. I know that you . . . have a glorious destiny.

JESUS: It may seem so.

MARY: (*Bursting out.*) I know that you are he who is come king of the Jews to save us! (*Any remaining crowd leaves, except the concealed* KLAUTUS.)

JESUS: (*Aware of crowd leaving.*) You think only in terms of this bit of earth. You do not know the whole work of salvation.

MARY: (*Almost exhausted from daring.*) We are oppressed.

JESUS: You are worse than that. You are oppressing. You are oppressing everyone who must lead you.

MARY: It is your burden and your destiny that oppress.

JESUS: You have read enough books to learn to express yourself. You have not read enough to understand one book.

MARY: Is this how you honor your mother?

JESUS: I honor you enough to speak the truth to you.

MARY: (*Agonizingly confused at her failure.*) Not all. You hold some back. You hint at secrets and mysteries and you will not tell them. Look at your poor puzzled disciples.

JESUS: They were not puzzled.

MARY: They were, they were, you would not see. You have led them away from all they know. And now, having made them homeless vagabonds, now you tell us it was just a little joke, a vacation, and now we can all go back to our bondage, and the vision of the Kingdom was a dream!

JESUS: (*Horrified at the thought.*) There is no truth in this.

MARY: Then what is truth? The truth is there are millions waiting for you to tell them: "Arise! Strike off your shackles! Follow me!" And "Lead us! Lead us!" is their cry, whatever they may say. And you lead them this far and no farther. And they must find their way back home in the dark over trails your words have wiped out.

JESUS: (*Spinning to see* PETER *and* JUDAS.) Peter. Judas. Is this true?

PETER: (*Angry, upset, but staunch.*) Lord,I have no doubts of you, nor no complaints of your teaching. I am a better man for it. and happier forever.

JESUS: (*To* PETER *at first, then to* MARY.) That is the very basis of all that I have said. Simply that. No more than that. Not to ask others for . . . sacrifice, but to find within yourself the seed of happiness.

MARY: A slave's bliss. Make the people happy. Teach the slaves to laugh and sing.

JESUS: (*Finding his strength in* PETER's *eyes.*) If that is more than they have known before.

MARY: And how shall the world be run then?

JESUS: (*His peace regained. Firmly.*) I know nothing of these matters.

JUDAS: Then who is to know? Who is to tell us? Rome?

JESUS: Judas!

MARY: (*To* JESUS, indicating JUDAS.) There? You see?

JESUS: (*Seeking inspiration. Beautifully.*) Judas. The kingdom of earth is like . . . like a man who has found a jewel in a fish, a great jewel that would serve him all his days, yet with that jewel he only goes and buys all the fish on the strand and tears them open, neither eating them nor selling them for gain, looking again for the jewel he has already sold away. But I say to you, the kingdom of heaven is beyond doubt, for he who finds it know it, and is content.

JUDAS: I see. Then do you mean that we should stay as we are born?

MARY: And he who sees this kingdom of heaven go away from him?

PETER: (*Moved and reaffirmed by the parable.*) It does not go.

MARY: (*Bitterly.*) I thought that I had found it in my son. And now I know that I was wrong.

JESUS: (*In despair of reaching her.*) Mother, you cannot find it in another. It is in you, only in you.

JUDAS: But . . . it seems to me that *I* have found it in you, my Lord.

JESUS: (*Nothing is working.*) Judas, I have only *helped* you find it.

MARY: (*Exploding.*) Find what? Peace? Is he at peace? (*Points at* JUDAS.) Is he? (*Points at* PETER.) Are the multitudes? All asking themselves "Why does he babble at us? When will he lead us? When will he tell us 'Take back what is ours!'?" Are *they* at peace? (*Moving in for the kill.*) Are *you*, Jesus of Nazareth?

JESUS: I was!

MARY: (*Melting, coddling, hypnotizing.*) Oh, yes, yes, yes, my son, you were! I have seen how, whenever you accept that glorious role, whenever you set one foot out on that road, you are at peace. Then and only then do your doubts cease, your burdens lift, your self-questionings no longer torture you, only when you accept that role! (JESUS *stands straight and tall to resist her. Then pity overtakes him.*)

JESUS: And I say to you that you do not know all of that role or you you would bite your tongue out before you speak. Mother, I have not forgotten what you sent me out to do; I have discovered something better. No. Listen. Pray with us. Our father who art in heaven . . . (PETER *and* JUDAS *kneel with* JESUS *at* JESUS' *gesture.*)

MARY: Which father? Abraham? Moses? Joseph the carpenter?

JESUS, JUDAS, PETER: Hallowed be thy name . . .

MARY: Is it "Tiberius"?

JESUS, JUDAS, PETER: Thy kingdom come . . .

MARY: Oh, it has come!

JESUS, JUDAS, PETER: Thy will be done . . .

MARY: It is being done while we dawdle here!

JESUS, JUDAS, PETER: On earth as it is in heaven.

MARY: Come one, come all, hear Jesus, the Roman astrologer!

JESUS, JUDAS, PETER: Give us this day our daily bread . . .

MARY: Beg Tiberius for the fruits of our own land!

JESUS, JUDAS, PETER: And forgive us our trespasses as we forgive those who trespass against us . . .

MARY: Yes, if we don't fight back, maybe they won't beat us any more!

JESUS, JUDAS, PETER: And lead us not into temptation . . .

MARY: You don't have to; we are walking into it gladly!

JESUS, JUDAS, PETER: But deliver us from evil . . .

MARY: Only he can, for he is the father of evil!

JESUS, JUDAS, PETER: For thine is the kingdom . . .

MARY: Rome!

JESUS, JUDAS, PETER: And the power . . .

MARY: The sword!

JESUS, JUDAS, PETER: And the glory . . .

MARY: All praise Tiberius!

JESUS, JUDAS, PETER: Forever . . .

MARY: Forever?

JESUS, JUDAS, PETER: And ever . . .

MARY: And ever?

JESUS: Amen!

MARY: Amen, so be it! You tell us to suffer and die gladly, Jesus. And will *you?*

JESUS: Oh, God that forgave in Eden the mortal greed for too much knowledge; God that forgave Cain his hatred of his brother's way of worship; God that forbade the hand of Abraham to sacrifice his son; God that forgave the murderers of Joseph and let him live to save his people; God that forgave all sins but the sin of Moses, who heard your clear command and disobeyed; God, poison me with her pain forever, yes, but forgive your daughter in her afflicted ignorance!

MARY: You say this to me, who taught you?

JESUS: (*Arising, confronting her like a new creature.*) Taught me? You do not know! I know now that you *do not know!*

MARY: I know the sound a crown makes when it falls on a marble floor is *King! King! King!* for all to hear!

JESUS: You speak of a crown on my head when what I feel is nails in my hands!

MARY: You're insane! You're insane! I don't know what you're talking about! I don't know why you're wasting time! I know there is a world waiting! And I know that's all I'm going to know because you won't tell me any more! I leave you to your disciples! It's up to them to make you see the light! (*She gathers her luggage.*)

JESUS: I have seen the light I want to see. I have seen it in their eyes when I speak of peace! (PETER *and* JUDAS *have, of course, been growing more and more visibly upset.* MARY *looks at them, sees their state, and calls* JESUS' *attention to them.*)

MARY: (*With strength and simplicity.*) And do you see it now? Do you? Or do you see doubt and fear? Ask them Jesus, ask them if you are leaving them in the light. And you men, if you care for him, tell him what is in your hearts. I know. It has always been in mine. I can say no more to you, Jesus. I leave you to your disciples. See if they are satisfied with what you say. (*She exits.*)

JESUS: (*Stung by doubt.*) Are you, Peter? Are you? Are you content?

PETER: (*Rising.*) I have said so. I can say no more.

JESUS: And you, Judas?

JUDAS: (*Rising; slowly, reluctantly.*) I hear the people talking in the streets, and I must say they say all that this woman, your mother, has been saying. And some answer as you have answered, and some answer as Peter, and some . . .

JESUS: Yes, Judas?

JUDAS: (*It comes out almost against his will.*) And some are in themselves twisted and complex. The light you have shed reveals the darkness in them, and all that was hidden in it, and for such as them there seems no redemption.

JESUS: Redemption from what?

JUDAS: (*Simply, still trusting.*) I don't know. That is what I hoped you might tell me.

JESUS: (*Looking after* MARY.) Then I *have* failed you?

JUDAS: No, no, I didn't mean that. Not for anything would I be without the things I've learned from you, only . . .

JESUS: (*"Come on, let's have it."*) Only what, Judas? I need for you to speak.

JUDAS: (*With contrasting violence.*) Only . . . what shall I do from day to day? How shall I live my life? What of this world? It matters much to me to know that I am doing what I should do, fulfilling in my days some plan I know is right. Who can tell us what to do? I know that you have given us commandments: you say, "Love one another."

JESUS: (*Correcting him.*) "Love one another *as you love yourself.*"

JUDAS: But what if love of one conflicts with love of another? What shall I do? Which shall I choose? How shall I choose? I cannot take a single loaf of bread and feed a multitude as they say you can.

JESUS: Judas, no. . . .

JUDAS: And even if you can't either, what can you do? What can I do? You say your kingdom is not of this earth, but this earth, here, now, is where we are. You've never needed anyone, you've never doubted yourself, but the rest of us—we need someone to show us the way. (*He is an image of helplessness and trust.*)

JESUS: (*Aware of danger. Very carefully.*) Judas, if I say to you that you must bear that anguish—and all the anguish that is in this world, and that I can only give you an example of peace within, that I can only show you that one can endure all pain of mind and body and spirit that the world can offer—and yet go on—then what would you say?

JUDAS: Then I would follow it.

JESUS: And why?

JUDAS: For love of you.

JESUS: (*One last agony of emotion.*) But I have come not that you should love me, but that you should love the kingdom of heaven.

JUDAS: But I find it in you, Lord; only in you.

JESUS: (*With distant logic.*) Then I have gone too far, and not far enough. Is that the case?

JUDAS: I'm not sure what you mean.

JESUS: There is a way that I began.

JUDAS: Show us the way. That is all I ask. If there is a way, show us.

JESUS: (*On the brink; one last little plea.*) Peter?

PETER: (*Who has been watching with growing confusion.*) I have been content with what I know . . . If there is more, then I will be glad to learn it. (JUDAS *and* PETER *are standing watching* JESUS. JESUS *smiles, closes his eyes, nods, clenches his fists, takes a deep breath and speaks as if speaking the solution to a complex mathematical problem.*)

JESUS: Everyone will be glad. They say they will. Everyone will be glad if they can know the end of the way. And all I ever wanted was that everyone should be glad. (*With quiet decision.*) Come to me. (PETER *and* JUDAS *move to him. He stops them.*) Not now. Tonight. We will be together. All will be revealed. All is well. Leave me alone now for a little while. Come to me again at suppertime. (*He exits.*)

PETER: I've never seen him like this. I didn't know he could be like this. We should follow him. (*But he looks to* JUDAS *for confirmation.*)

JUDAS: (*With great peace and authority.*) No, he told us not to.

> PILATE *enters his office from his private rooms, holding books which he is checking. He exits off to* KLAUTUS's *office.*

PETER: But I think he needs us.

> PILATE *re-enters with another book and a sheaf of forms, sits down at his desk and rather merrily proceeds to fill out forms.*

JUDAS: I have something to do. Someone who's been kind to me that I should . . . tell goodbye. I should have done it before.

PETER: What do you think he's going to tell us tonight?

JUDAS: I don't know. (*Noticing* PETER's *confusion.*) But he said that all would be made clear. He wouldn't lie to us. Oh, don't look sad, Peter. He promised. He promised, Peter. He promised. (JUDAS *exits.* PETER *exits.* KLAUTUS *comes out from hiding, gazes after* JESUS, *and exits on the run.*)

SCENE TWO

PILATE's *office, shortly afterwards.* PILATE *is onstage at his desk, writing official little documents, checking books for data, whistling. He is quite cheery.* KLAUTUS, *still in streetclothes, enters up center, stands staring at* PILATE's *back for a moment, then clears his throat.*

PILATE: (*Barely looking up.*) Well, back at last. And what have you accomplished?

KLAUTUS: Well, I have seen him, my lord.

PILATE: (*Still working.*) You have seen your lord?

KLAUTUS: No sir. I have seen the streets. You are my lord.

PILATE: The streets, Klautus, are both our lords. But have you seen the new prophet?

KLAUTUS: I have, lord. Sir.

PILATE: And? What does he say?

KLAUTUS: He says . . . many things, sir.

PILATE: Well, he *must* be gifted if he is so eloquent as to leave you dumb. Tell me what you remember, what struck you.

KLAUTUS: Well, he said . . . many things.

PILATE: (*Impatient but amused. Supplying words.*) But it was his manner of saying them?

KLAUTUS: (*Buoyant.*) Oh, yes. He spoke ... better than beautifully. Almost as well as you, sir. (*Pause. Bravely.*) I don't think he's dangerous, sir. He said all men are brothers.

PILATE: (*Interested in the effect on* KLAUTUS.) Did he, now?

KLAUTUS: And that we are all part of one kingdom.

PILATE: But what kingdom?

KLAUTUS: Only the kingdom of god, sir.

PILATE: What god?

KLAUTUS: (*"Oh, dear."*) He was not specific, sir.

PILATE: Good. What else?

KLAUTUS: (*Definitely defending* JESUS. *Leans on desk.*) Well, virtually nothing that was in any way whatsoever even remotely political, sir. He said pay taxes. He said obey the law.

PILATE: Did he, indeed?

KLAUTUS: He said not to think too much on this world.

PILATE: Ever-welcome advice. Go on.

KLAUTUS: And then he said, privately, in conversation to your Judas, he said—well—many things. There were two others there, a man called Peter—one of his very close ones—and a woman who was his mother.

PILATE: A mother. Go on.

KLAUTUS: His speech became confused. Judas was very troubled, like last night, asking questions.

PILATE: You listened.

KLAUTUS: You ordered me to.

PILATE: Last night?

KLAUTUS: (*"Uh-oh!"*) Oh ... (*Snaps to attention worriedly.*)

PILATE: (*Laughs.*) Go ahead, boy, I'm teasing you. I haven't said a word since I was twenty that couldn't be heard by the whiole world. Go on.

KLAUTUS: Well ... then there was some talk of a King of the Jews. They tried to make him say he was the one.

PILATE: Oh, now we come to it.

KLAUTUS: (*Quickly.*) But he did not. Even when they tried to make him say it.

PILATE: Poor man. And what else?

KLAUTUS: (*Watching* PILATE *cautiously.*) They talked some more, but that was all the sense I made of it.

PILATE: (*Wanders to the window.*) Good enough. And what do they say in the streets?

KLAUTUS: Much the same, sir. But with much quarreling among the different religions. (*Wearily.*) I mean the different parts of the one religion. Do you know what I mean?

PILATE: (*With depth.*) So very well.

KLAUTUS: (*Conscientious, then excited.*) And rumors that he does miracles. And that he is the son of God, like Caesar. (*Wooooops!*) I'm only telling you what I heard, sir. (*Attention.*) As you asked me to. Ordered me to.

PILATE: (*Advancing toward him.*) Treason! And heresy! (KLAUTUS *thinks he is being charged and closes his eyes and waits for death.*) And madness and civic unrest! (*Suddenly lightly.*) Goodness! I think it is time that we—what is it they call it?—oh, yes, "capture" this young man and "persecute" him. (*All business. Takes a document from the desk and gives it to* KLAUTUS.) Go get the captain of the guard for me. Poor fool.

KLAUTUS: (*Reprieved; puzzled.*) Who, sir? I? (JUDAS *enters up center behind* KLAUTUS.)

PILATE: (*Delighted and surprised.*) Judas!

KLAUTUS: (*Shocked.*) Judas is a poor fool? (*Then he sees* JUDAS.)

PILATE: (*To* KLAUTUS.) Out with you, boy! (KLAUTUS *exits.*) Judas! You are just in time. Tonight it is I who need *your* help.

JUDAS: (*A little afraid, but bravely resolved.*) Pilate, I came to ask you to free me from your service.

PILATE: (*Raises his eyebrows.*) You are not in my service, Judas, but in my care. Do you wish to be free of my care?

JUDAS: I think I am not fit for the post you are training me for.

PILATE: I think you are most fit. I have work for you tonight.

JUDAS: Not tonight.

PILATE: (*Somewhat coyly.*) The sooner the better, I think. This holy man—what's his name?

JUDAS: I don't know.

PILATE: (*Still playful.*) I am sure you do, Judas. Help me.

JUDAS: I can't. I don't know.

PILATE: (*Only slightly disciplinarian.*) I thought you would, Judas. You were with him today.

JUDAS: (*Quietly.*) Jesus?

PILATE: (*Playful again.*) That's the one. The one the streets are full for.

JUDAS: (*Forgetting his errand.*) What's happened? Has he been harmed?

PILATE: (*Somewhat archly.*) Not yet. I want you to bring him to me. (*Offers a document to* JUDAS.) There are terrible rumors.

JUDAS: (*Refusing document.*) My lord, he has done nothing wrong. He couldn't.

PILATE: I'm sure he hasn't, Judas, but there are those who would wrong *him.* He has acquired a political aroma.

JUDAS: He doesn't seek it. I swear he doesn't.

PILATE: I know the type, Judas. I believe you. But there is no one single Herod now to "persecute heresy."

JUDAS: He is not a heretic.

PILATE: (*Hurt and a little offended.*) Judas, I know. And I am not a persecutor. I thought this would please you. He has given twenty sects out there twenty reasons to murder him, and one of them is bound to do it. I want you to bring him here. (*Extends document again.*)

JUDAS: (*Refusing document.*) You thought it would please me to know that he is in danger?

PILATE: No, to know that I want to help him.

JUDAS: You help him?

PILATE: Certainly help him. What do you think I would want to do to a poor misled lamb like that? I'll give you a regiment of the guards. (*Makes* JUDAS *take order.*)

JUDAS: (*Throws order on table.*) You can't. I can't.

PILATE: (*Underestimating* JUDAS's *distrust.*) Judas, I can't go after him myself. He's said a few things Rome might take seriously if I do. He can't approach the palace alone, he'd be drawn and quartered. You're one of the people, they know you, I want you to fetch him here for safety.

JUDAS: Do you mean that?

PILATE: (*He is trying to be tactful.*) Well, that and more ... I have been a student of your religion, Judas. . . . It has, like all religions, a dark and secret side—which is about to be revealed if we don't . . .

JUDAS: (*His fear only mounting.*) How do *you* know *that?*

PILATE: My dear boy, at the risk of frightening you, I have seen several dozen religions reach this particular boiling point. When a religion rots it reveals its skeleton. A faith as ancient as yours accumulates a mass of mystic, cabalistic tradition known only to a select few.

JUDAS: Like yourself?

PILATE: (*Stung.*) Judas, that is one of the things we are trying to do away with.

JUDAS: (*With adult anger.*) Then *tell me* what you are *talking about.*

PILATE: (*Shocked off-guard.*) I'd really rather not if I don't have to, Judas!

KLAUTUS: (*Enters in military garb. Clicks heels.*) The captain of the guard is here, sir.

PILATE: (*Angrily.*) Have him wait. Get out.

KLAUTUS: (*With heel click.*) Yes, sir! (*Exits.*)

PILATE: (*Recovering his composure.*) Where was I?

JUDAS: Secrets. Secrets, spies, soldiers, and secrets.

PILATE: (*Recovered.*) Ah, yes. Well, it seems your Jesus has, advertently or inadvertently, fulfilled in his public actions some old prophecies of your people. He has—oh—entered Jerusalem in a certain sort of procession, made those claims at the Temple, etcetera, all of which adds up to . . . (*He looks at* JUDAS's *angry suspicious face and looks away. One would think he was hedging.*) one thing.

JUDAS: Yes, what? Where does it lead?

PILATE: Well, it relates to the coming of a hero, a savior of the people, presumably, in this case, their savior from Roman domination and the destruction of the True Faith.

JUDAS: Oh, I've heard those prophecies all my life; we all know those prophecies.

PILATE: Yes. Well. Your high priest, Caiaphas, has, like me, observed the young man's rather theatrical assumption of this role, and assumes that . . . Jesus . . . wishes to carry out the remainder of the . . . ritual, prophecy, whatever one wants to call it. So! I want you to bring him here. (*Extends document again, falsely cheerful.*)

JUDAS: (*Refusing document.*) But what is the . . . remainder of the ritual?

PILATE: It's rather frightening, Judas, so let's just . . . (*Extends document.*)

JUDAS: (*With undisguised accusation.*) No more frightening than deception and spies and secrecy!

PILATE: (*Really angry. With tight lips.*) You think not? Well! It seems there is a . . . sacrifice involved.

JUDAS: (*Uncomprehending.*) Sacrifice?

PILATE: (*Instantly regretful.*) Yes, yes, I'm sorry for frightening you. A sacred execution. Apparently our Roman custom of crucifixion fills the scriptural specifications admirably. A human lamb to be slain at the same time as the Passover lamb. Something your more radical political occultists have distilled out of the books you call Exodus and Hosea and Isaiah and Zechariah and other ancient scribblings.

JUDAS: (*On whom it has been growing.*) Sacrifice? And tomorrow?

PILATE: (*Not happy.*) Yes. I told you it was not pretty.

JUDAS: (*Oblivious of* PILATE.) Then . . . *that* was what he was talking about?

PILATE: (*Not without distaste.*) Oh. So he is aware of it?

JUDAS: (*On guard again.*) I don't know. For certain.

PILATE: Let me help you. Has he had himself . . . anointed?

JUDAS: Anointed? The other day at Bethany some woman poured this expensive ointment over him. I thought it was foolishness, but he said . . . he said . . . he said he would not be among us long. . . .

PILATE: (*Gently.*) The word for this savior is "Messiah." In Greek it is "Christos." Both words mean "anointed."

JUDAS: (*Danger on all sides.*) I still don't know, for certain, if he means to do . . . what you said.

PILATE: (*Trying to be chatty.*) Well, if he does, Judas, it would put Caiaphas in a position to do untold annoyance under the guise— or for all I know, the sincere intention—of reuniting the factions of Judaism and . . . cause a great deal of trouble.

JUDAS: For Rome?

PILATE: (*Urbanity to the winds.*) For everyone, Judas. Rebellion. Riots. Ugly arrests. The execution of the unbelieving. The restoration in a modern metropolitan environment of totally unsuitable agricultural religious rites. The confusion and subjugation of the people under a degraded regime that cannot possibly fill their needs.

JUDAS: Their spiritual needs.

PILATE: Their spiritual needs, their bodily needs, their hearts, their brains, their bellies. Lord, when did the mind and body become so separated that they require separate saviors? Come, let us have a little humor about this. I've seen it happen, Judas, time after time; I'm sick of it. You have seen just recently your John the Baptist, a fine mind wasted by outmoded irrelevant marriage taboos, when there are roads to build with such a mind, laws to clarify, grain to transport around the world from where it is grown to where it is needed. I'm sick of it, I'm tired of it, I've learned to turn my back on it, but this one time I thought I might interfere. (*Smiles at* JUDAS, *not without strain.*)

JUDAS: And will you . . . what, then . . . kill Caiaphas?

PILATE: (*Genuinely surprised. Laughs.*) Good heavens, no! He's only a cat's-paw in your Jesus' game. You and I—we—will persuade Jesus to live!

JUDAS: He is against all factions.

PILATE: I am against all factions, too, Judas, including his.

JUDAS: He will never preach your religion.

PILATE: (*Angry at rejection and somewhat insulted.*) Oh, let him preach what he will. We don't care what religious games you play as long as you don't play them in the traffic! All we can say as you stagger out of your various temples is, "Here. Here is law and order, clean and wholesome." We simply don't want men torn between conflicting kingdoms.

JUDAS: The kingdom of this earth?

PILATE: The only one there is, Judas! Where else shall goodness or evil manifest themselves but in the affairs of men? Let me tell you something: there are no gods, Judas, no ghosts; the only consciousness in the cosmos is the men and women who are alive right now. The universe will be as sane or as insane as we are.

JUDAS: You all keep telling me that what I feel, this wreckage and confusion, is only within me? And you think that will make me feel better?

PILATE: (*Ultimately with tenderness.*) It is inside any man who lives in division from all others, Judas. Here, look, hold up your palm to mine. See? You are here, I am here, you are a man, I am a man, we are alike, but different. There are some things we both need: food, clothing, shelter, water, mates, a place to feed our waste, words to speak of sensible matters, practical rules to help us about our business. The other things, the things that are inside a man—that is his private kingdom.

JUDAS: But there are other things that people need!

PILATE: (*A little disappointed.*) Yes, yes, gods, art, we have spoken of those things . . .

JUDAS: (*With surprising power.*) Don't treat me like a child, Pilate, don't smile at me! We are not speaking here of gods and art! We are speaking of men. There are other things that men seem to need to do. They kill and rob. They murder and they torture. They quarrel in their streets and in their senates. They will say anything to win others to their causes. They plot. And they deceive. And . . . (*Admitting it.*) they sacrifice.

PILATE: Yes, Judas. Yes. We all have those things within us. You have them. I have them. We simply don't do them. Unless reason fails.

JUDAS: And if reason fails . . .

PILATE: (*Turning away.*) If reason fails, then perhaps it is reason's fault, yes.

JUDAS: Don't talk philosophy at me! That is not what I was going to say! If reason fails, then what do we do?

PILATE: We fight and survive. Or we turn the other cheek and perish.

JUDAS: He said that, "Turn the other cheek."

PILATE: I know. I have his sayings on my desk.

JUDAS: He says that we *must* turn the other cheek.

PILATE: (*Implacable.*) Then why is he doing this heartless act of war against Rome?

JUDAS: (*After long pause. Unemotionally.*) You want me to bring this man to you?

PILATE: (*Extending order.*) Please.

JUDAS: For Rome's sake.

PILATE: (*Breaking.*) For Rome's protection. You're making all this much too significant, Judas. Let me save him for you. It is of less than no importance to me. I only wanted to show you that, with Rome, it could be done.

JUDAS: I think you may be right—about what he means to do. (*Takes order.*) I will bring him to you. I have to trust someone.

PILATE: (*Quietly. Honorably.*) Is there any reason why you should not trust me?

JUDAS: No. No. None at all. I may have been very foolish.

PILATE: Judas, I am aware that this man is very strong and . . . very moving to his followers.

JUDAS: Yes, he is that.

PILATE: I am not asking you to choose between him and . . . anything.

JUDAS: I know that you do not mean to. Everyone tells me I do not have to make a choice. But everyone who tells me that has already chosen.

PILATE: Let us help him to choose to live and make a better world.

JUDAS: I am tired. You have given me my orders.

PILATE: I have asked you.

JUDAS: You have asked me. He has asked me to supper. I will show your soldiers the place. I will . . . kiss him . . . to show that he is the one.

PILATE: Is that a custom among them?

JUDAS: Yes.

PILATE: Very well. And, Judas . . .

JUDAS: Yes?

PILATE: By all means, let him know what we are doing. (*Gives* JUDAS *another order.*) Tell him the guards are under his command.

JUDAS: I will tell him . . . what I was told. (*Trying to make amends.*) He said today that you . . . were of the kingdom of God.

PILATE: I will not presume on that.

JUDAS: He said you served him, in your way.

PILATE: I hope that I serve life and order. (KLAUTUS *enters in full uniform.* PILATE *hands him the remaining orders from the desk.*)

JESUS *enters below. He is clearly troubled, but in silent communion with some other voice. He nods, growing calmer and more resolute.*

JUDAS: May I go now?

PETER: (*Off, below.*) Jesus! Jesus! (JESUS *turns toward* PETER'S *voice. He looks up, as if listening, smiles, nods.*)

PILATE: Certainly. Come. I will take you myself to the captain of the guard. (PILATE *and* JUDAS *exit together.* PILATE *plucks an order from* KLAUTUS's *hand in passing.* KLAUTUS, *highly offended, follows.*)

SCENE THREE

A garden. JESUS *turns to smile at* PETER.

PETER: Lord, wait. I want to talk to you.

JESUS: (*Calmer than the moonlight.*) Wait, Peter. We must wait for Judas. (*Looks off for* JUDAS.)

PETER: But that's what I want to ask you, is what you meant about Judas. I can't understand. None of us understand.

JESUS: Not yet, Peter, no, not yet. (*He moves away.*)

JUDAS: (*Entering.*) Peter, leave him alone, please.

PETER: (*Looking for help from anyone.*) But what does he mean? What was he saying in there? Why does he have us celebrating Passover a day early?

JUDAS: There isn't time, Peter, you'll understand.

PETER: But it was crazy! "Drink my blood"? "Eat my body"? "This is the last time we will be together"? What is he *saying?*

JUDAS: (*As if to a child, with difficulty.*) He may not know what he's saying, Peter. All right?

PETER: (*With growing dread.*) He said you'd betray him. You work for the Romans.

JUDAS: We all work for the Romans, if we work at all.

PETER: I won't listen to you. (*Turns to* JESUS.) Lord, what has Judas done to you?

JESUS: (*Who has heard, if at all, with a calm smile.*) Be at peace. Be at peace.

PETER: (*Instantly dubious of his fears.*) But ... some of the things you said in there. (*Sheepish.*) You scared me.

JUDAS: (*Tries to draw* PETER *away.*) Peter, don't ...

PETER: (*Flings* JUDAS *away.*) I want to ask him about the things he *said!* (*Turns again to* JESUS.)

JESUS: (*Undisturbed.*) Please. There is no need to ask, Peter. All will be revealed. Judas?

JUDAS: Yes, Lord.

JESUS: All that you told me earlier? For tonight?

JUDAS: (*Earnestly.*) Yes, Lord.

PETER: (*Jealous, frightened.*) What? What about tonight?

JESUS: (*Almost laughing at them.*) No, no, all will be revealed. We will do as you said, Judas.

JUDAS: Yes, please.

PETER: Am I to know nothing, Lord?

JESUS: (*With parental tolerance.*) Everyone will know everything, every step of the way. Now listen quietly. I may never speak to you again. (*Quieting their protests.*) No, listen. We will do now what I set out to do. When I said that all would be revealed, I did not mean that I would *tell* you. You will see. Each of us has a part that he must play out, tonight, and tomorrow, and ... however long it lasts.

PETER: (*Again, somewhat calmed.*) Well, of course, Lord, whatever you say.

JESUS: I have told you one of you will betray me.

JUDAS: Lord ...

PETER: (*Instantly upset again.*) But Judas has sworn that he will not. Is he lying?

JUDAS: (*"I give up."*) Oh, never mind, Peter.

JESUS: I know, I know, I know much more than I can tell you now. You will be shown.

JUDAS: (*"Let's give it a try."*) Lord, forgive me if I speak. I would not claim to know more than you, but if there are some things that you have not experienced that I have ...

JESUS: I have experienced all I came for. All but the last.

JUDAS: (*Failure.*) Of course, Lord.

PETER: And I, Lord?

JESUS: Ah, yes, you. You will deny me, Peter.

PETER: (*As if accused.*) Never!

JESUS: (*A sly smile coming over his face.*) Peter, not even if I say you will?

PETER: (*Nothing makes any sense.*) You are telling me to deny you?

JESUS: (*Smile growing.*) No. I am only saying that you will. Three times you will deny me as in the prophecy.

PETER: (*This is impossible.*) But I won't.

JESUS: (*Tenderness coming into the smile.*) Peter, if you do not, then I am a false prophet.

PETER: (*Stopped.*) I cannot answer such a thing as that.

JESUS: (*Almost laughing with loving tenderness.*) I know. Trust me that I know. Remember, (*To* JUDAS.) you will betray me. (*To* PETER.) You will deny me. Three times. Judas, you will be offered a reward.

JUDAS: They pay me at the palace, Lord, how else should I live? But a reward . . .

JESUS: No, another will reward you. The price—the price of a slave—was set long ago.

JUDAS: Reward, what a word.

JESUS: Sh. Judas, I want to go and pray now. (JUDAS *moves to him.*) No, alone. I will go out in the garden, if I may, and pray alone. Then you will come and we will do as I said. May I? Have the time to go and pray?

JUDAS: Whatever you say, Lord, always.

JESUS: Not so long. Oh, not nearly so long. Let me go now. I will not be long. And Peter . . .

PETER: Yes, Lord.

JESUS: (*With growing seriousness and dignity.*) Peter. Judas. You are like two little caged doves, fretting and moaning to be free. Do not be afraid. I am not here to bring you pain. You will be with me. Someday. Yes. You will all be with me someday. I only go before to prepare for you. You will follow me. This is not the end. You will all follow me. I go before you, but I only go to prepare rooms for you in my father's house. (*He exits.*)

PETER: (*After a moment. Turning on* JUDAS.) What are you up to? How will you betray him?

JUDAS: He has misunderstood.

PETER: (*Vehemently.*) If he says I will deny him, then he has.

JUDAS: (*"How did I get into this?"*) Oh, or you have, or I have, don't worry, I promise you, everything will be made clear.

PETER: He said that.

JUDAS: And I say it. God, now I know how they feel. It will be all right, Peter, you will know.

PETER: I know that I will never doubt him.

JUDAS: (*With superiority.*) Oh, if you are never to doubt him, then I must betray him and you must deny him. Now think about that and let us go protect him! (*Starts off.*)

PETER: (*Refusing to follow.*) Who do you think you are to start giving the rest of us orders?

JUDAS: (*With bitter humor.*) I? I am the wisest person in the world, Peter, because they know everything, and I know them. Oh, come, let's get the others and go look after him. (JUDAS *exits the opposite way from* JESUS.)

KLAUTUS: *above, enters* PILATE's *office and goes straight through to* PILATE's *private chambers.*

PETER: Oh, Lord, please take away this task that you have laid upon me.

PILATE: (*Off.*) What?

PETER: No, you named me "Peter," "Petrus," "Stone." You said that you would build your church upon me.

PILATE: (*Enters from his chambers, outraged, in tux.*) I am experiencing great difficulty in believing what you are telling me, Klautus!

KLAUTUS: (*Entering from* PILATE's *chambers.*) It is only what I am told, sir.

PETER: Whatever is to come, whatever happens. In this, and in all things, your will . . .

PILATE: He has been before Caiaphas? At this time of night?

PETER: Your will . . .

KLAUTUS: Not only before Caiaphas, sir, but before the whole college of priests.

PETER: Your will, by me, by everyone, be done. (PETER *exits after*
JUDAS.)

SCENE FOUR

PILATE*'s office. Night.* PILATE *is staring at* KLAUTUS.

PILATE: (*Coldly.*) It's called the Sanhedrin.

KLAUTUS: Yes sir.

PILATE: Well, Caiaphas has gone a bit too far this time. How dare
he delay a detachment of the Roman Guard?

KLAUTUS: (*Helping* PILATE *finish dressing.*) He—Caiaphas did
not, sir.

PILATE: Caiaphas did not what?

KLAUTUS: You put the guard under the orders of the prophet, sir.
It was he who told the guard to take him before the, uh . . .

PILATE: (*Dead.*) Sanhedrin.

KLAUTUS: Sanhedrin.

PILATE: Through the streets, before the Sanhedrin. Before a great
crowd, no doubt?

KLAUTUS: So I am told.

PILATE: "Sir."

KLAUTUS: Sir.

PILATE: And what state is he in now?

KLAUTUS: He ordered the soldiers to bind him, sir.

PILATE: I have no doubt whatsoever that they obeyed.

KLAUTUS: They are good Roman soldiers, sir.

PILATE: Caiaphas no doubt made sure that all the crowd heard the
necessary allegations against the young man.

KLAUTUS: It would seem so. Sir.

PILATE: So, instead of a quiet troop of discreet soldiers and an
endangered holy man, I have, out in my courtyard . . .

KLAUTUS: (*Wheeling out a cart of wine, water, cigarettes, fruit, etc.*) A
great crowd of religious persons, soldiers holding them back,
quite a large percentage of the common folk, and a few of his
followers, sir. (*It should be pointed out here that at no time in this
scene, until his leavetaking, does* KLAUTUS *betray any emotion whatsoever.*)

PILATE: Oh, God. He's going to win, he's going to win, he'll thrust
that cross into Golgotha like a conqueror's claiming sword! All
right, bring him in.

KLAUTUS: Did you want your Judas as well, sir?

PILATE: No, I'll apologize to him later. Leave the soldiers outside. Leave the priests outside. Barricade the palace from the people, and let the disciples wait. Send the damned brilliant nuisance in! (KLAUTUS *hesitates.*) Well, send him in!

KLAUTUS: Sir?

PILATE: More surprises?

KLAUTUS: (*At attention, not looking* PILATE *in the eyes.*) Sir, you do not intend to harm him, sir?

PILATE: Not unless he has arranged it unavoidably. GET OUT! (KLAUTUS *exits very fast. We hear only a trailing "Yes sir."*) Oh, Lord. Maybe Herod couldn't *help* killing John. (KLAUTUS *re-enters with* JESUS, *whose hands are bound together with coarse rope.*)

KLAUTUS: The prophet Jesus, sir, called King of the Jews.

PILATE: (*Shocked at* JESUS' *appearance. Angry.*) Get out, boy. Leave us alone. And by that I mean alone. Go to all the little spyholes you and the others have dug and drag them away. Or by my name, somebody will be crucified tomorrow. Do you hear me?

KLAUTUS: (*Heel-click.*) Yes *sir!* (Exits. PILATE *and* JESUS *are alone.* JESUS *has barely entered the room. He does not know where he is or what might be about to happen to him.* PILATE *instantly recovers himself and becomes genial and even conspiratorial.*)

PILATE: Forgive me for just one moment. I have to check every nook and cranny of this torture chamber. (*He looks for peepholes, etc.*) I think they must have planted coiled tubes so they can cluster in the basement and overhear great matters. As if great matters were different from their own lives, no? As if *we* were some sort of superior creature. Oh, here, let me take those ropes off of you.

(*He goes to* JESUS, *hands out.* JESUS *turns, or moves, away.*)

How could you do such a thing? I am surprised at you. You have been in those streets all your life, you know what those people are, how they will take this. Of course you do. You have had to speak to them in parables and poetry. Let me unbind you and offer an understanding hand in friendship.

(*Again he tries to unbind* JESUS. JESUS *turns away.*)

Well. I don't blame you. You know what you're about. I must say, you might have made this easier on me. That rope may have made a great hit with your followers and foes, but I will hear about it from Rome, believe me. Won't you sit down? Here is wine, and fruit, and water. I should have you served, but I do wish to speak with you in private, so I must ask that you refresh yourself.

(JESUS *turns away.* PILATE *is struck with a thought.*)

No? Oh, God, I see I must reassure you. You are not a captive. You are not brought here to be persecuted. This is not *your* torture chamber, it is *mine.* You heard those people in the streets? Some of them have been out there for days, demanding that I do to you what they no doubt believe I am now doing.

Had I not offered you my protection, they would, believe me, be doing it to you themselves. They have been besieging me, beseeching me, in ever-growing numbers, to get rid of you.

(*Laughs.*)

And the motives, the variety of motives.

(*As if telling a long, complicated joke.*)

Some say you are a terrorist, threatening to tear the temple down. And the penalty for terrorism is . . . death.

Some say you are a magician, raising the dead. And the penalty for the practice of magic is . . . death.

Some say you are a diabolist, communing with the devils they believe you cast out. And the penalty for diabolism is . . . death.

Some say you are sacrilegious, interfering with the Passover sacrifices. And the penalty for sacrilege is . . . death.

Some say you are seditious against the Sanhedrin, flouting the Sabbath laws, etcetera. And the penalty for such sedition is . . . death.

Some say you are an idolater, claiming to *be* the object of worship. And the penalty for idolatry is . . . death.

Some say you have made yourself a Gentile by your heresies. And the penalty for a Gentile setting foot in the temple grounds is . . . death.

Some say you are a traitor against Rome, proclaiming yourself the rightful King of the Jews. And the penalty for treason against Rome *is* . . . death.

And some say you are guiltless, guileless, glorious, innocent, that you *are* the messiah, savior, king. And the confirmation of that claim must be your ritual, prophesied, sacramental, sacrificial . . . death!

How did you keep yourself hidden so long? Look what you have aroused now that you have come out in the open. You are a man of particular, spectacular power! You are what we dream of finding, of rewarding, a fine and vibrant mind, a dynamic person-

ality, a brilliant command of language. I have been reading your
sayings, your *Logia,* they are poetry.

Do you think that we are savages? Do you think that we
created those irresistible legions only to have them march you to
Golgotha? Do you think we taught them to follow to have
them follow you? You cannot think that!

The ability to survive—and this alone would mark you as
exceptional—the ability to survive intellectually when you have
obviously had that beautiful brain crammed to bursting with the
most noxious drivel that centuries of foaming visionaries could
hand down to you in a form as involved, as thoroughly mangled
and obscured as their own self-doubting, delirious visions of the
world . . .

(*He has lost his sentence, and his thought.*)

You are welcome here, in the home of clarity and light.
Rome—the world—your own people, if you see them as such—
need you. Look how you can reach them, look how they respond
to you. Can you doubt that if you told them the truth—the truth
you must know to know how to manipulate them so—that they
would begin with your help, with the help of Rome, to inch
themselves—yes, and Rome, too, for Rome has never pretended
to perfection—toward something better? It is not impossible
that you should *have* the throne of Judea, Jesus, Christ. Surely a
people are better regulated by one who knows their cradle-
songs. We can offer them, at best, an alien enlightenment. You
can guide them through a familiar darkness to it.

(JESUS *turns away.*)

It is not politics that entrances you? Then let us send you to
academies in Rome, where you may, for the first time, encounter
minds the equals of your own. You have been bred in such depri-
vation, with only the usual holy books of the usual true faith. It
will amaze you what you will find in Rome. How you will read
and see yourself mirrored in the martyrs of a million tiny sects.
But not completely mirrored, for *you* will step out of that dreary
peasant-dance and instead contribute to the greater order of
mankind—not threaten even its remnants. Or would you prefer
to be sent out beyond Judea, to new territory? Rome is expand-
ing, it will be one world, a Roman world. And you can help to
make that happen, help innocent, well-meaning men to avoid the
mistake that I hope I am helping you avoid . . .

(JESUS *turns away.*)

Jesus *please* sit. Rest yourself. Look at me, I am throwing too much at you at once. I forget you are a simple man, overlearned in one area perhaps, perhaps not even aware of the magnitude of opportunity.

What are you thinking, Jesus? What are you thinking? The workings of the mind are never simple. You think perhaps that it is enough merely to stand and speak the truth to simple people and they will understand, arise, and make man better? You wonder why we Romans do not simply stand and do that? But you see out there in the streets what they do when it is simply spoken to them! And are we so sure we even know the truth yet? If we did, then would not everything be working properly, perfectly, as perfectly as your plan to have yourself extinguished seems to be working out? Perhaps you know some one additional thing which, added to the immense awareness of Rome, could bring a perfect world about. With all the power of Rome behind you!

Jesus, the truth may be simple, but the people are not. They are not individuals out there, waving their hands and screaming "vengeance!" They are a complex like a beehive, and as predictable. They are each of them, like you, cells in a honeyhive of superstition. They are not young, they were never young. They were born as old as whatever swamp of a civilization they were born into. Every available convolution of their brains was stuffed at birth with the endlessly self-defeating presuppositions of cultures which have been, in all the experience of Rome, either bands of murderers waving god's name on a banner, or else sobbing slave-pools wailing their celestial superiority to their terrestrial torment, living in slavery, passing their young on into slavery, not even hesitating to have young: animals, worms, bugs, vegetables, toads! Is it for them you are willing to sacrifice yourself?

(JESUS *turns away.* PILATE *is aware he's gone overboard.*)

They need not be like that. Don't let me make you think they must. I have seen—besides these horrors—I have seen light come into the eyes of men. You have seen it, too, you stir. Yes, I have seen, right here in this office, I have seen a heart open, a mind take fire, the concept of beauty and truth kindled in a consciousness that had known only fear and dread. And you can do that, too, you can bring that about. The end of sorrow, the end of sacrifice—yes, that moves you, I can see it does—the end

of all insane exigencies ... (JESUS *turns away.*) But not by turning away from me!

Let me say one more thing to you. If you are afraid you have
been too poisoned, too tainted, to change your ways and work in
a world of men, do not think so. You can be saved. I know it is
hard. I have seen men shake off superstition and succumb to it
again and again. It is woven into your nursery rhymes, beaten
into you by your father, whined into you by your mother—
yes, you know about that, don't you?—but it is not by super-
natural insight that I know it, it is from simple experience, in all
countries, it has always been the same.

But not for all of us, don't despair, we survive, we survive,
without faith or hope we find a way, we few, to bear all the
anguish of the world and yet go on ...

(JESUS *turns away.*)

What was it? What did I say? I've made it seem too hard. But
look what you've borne already, Jesus, and from your own free
will! Now turn that will to something harder (*Laughs*), yes, a
million times harder, I admit it, but with hope at the end, not this
dreary descent into primeval muck!

(JESUS *turns away.* PILATE *grabs him and spins him around.*)

Do not turn away! I beg you! Let me help you! As you have
helped others, let me help you!

(*He releases* JESUS. JESUS *walks a few steps away.*)

Is it that you think you have set in motion something that
cannot be stopped? That may well be, Jesus, that may well be.
What schemes, Jesus, what schemes have you rigged, as you
rigged your entry into Jerusalem and your other secret fulfill-
ments of your cult's eschatology? And cleverly, I admit it, for
even with my interest in your faith, it took me until tonight to
see what Caiaphas perceived at once!

Oh, yes, he saw, he understood, he is ready to have you sacrificed now. Unless you publicly deny what you have never publicly claimed—unless you did it at that trial tonight—that you
are King of the Jews—then it is my hands, not yours, that are
tied. I must release you to the military police, and they will raise
you on a cross. Yes! Like the serpent that gathered the tribes
together in the desert! Every law and lariat, every slurping
mouthful of legalisms and spit is ready to send you reeling on to
your glorious end. Then my only concern will be to make it seem
Caiaphas' fault, and his to make it seem mine, and you will be

forgotten in our libraries of litigation! But perhaps that is what you wish for most, never even to have been, the immortality of oblivion. Well, if all you want is to have it over, then there it is, out there, you may die as effortlessly as you have lived, and with even more pain!

Maybe you're right! Maybe you should be crucified! Maybe you *should* be elevated above the earth where the common people root for solutions! Maybe *you're* what's *wrong* with the earth! (*He is at window, looks out and down, turns.*) Jesus, this is not belief! This is *beyond* belief! Do you think we want your suicide? Do you think we need *that?* Do you think anyone wants your death but you? Do you think your suffering is what we have thought, taught, fought, killed and built for? Civilizations are not labored over for the likes of you and me, Jesus, elevated upon our crosses and towers. Wars are fought for the mind of Judas! Philosophies founded for the peace of mind of Judas! Religions are permitted, allowances made, mythologies propounded, not that you and I may win and lose, but so that Judas may arise each morning knowing who he is and what his day's work on that day must be.

Jesus. The truths they tell against you are lies to kill you. Lie that you might live to tell the truth. Say you are not king of the Jews and live to be. Say you are not the son of God and live to show us that we all are. Say you are not the enemy of Rome and live to help destroy Rome—and rebuild it. Do you think you are alone up here? I know why you're doing this—and I know for whom. But we who sacrifice ourselves to systems we do not believe in merely to secure the happiness of others—we may be only creating our own destroyers!

I, above all—(*Laughs.*) above all!—I understand you feel you must sacrifice yourself. But those feelings are not your own thoughts. And these thoughts are not perhaps my own feelings! But I do devoutly believe that men can live without faith! (*Pauses.*) I . . . I know that sounds a schoolboy paradox. I . . . I know it sounds as if I am asking you, and Judas, and Klautus, and all the world, to live without a faith when I have . . . have had . . . have always had . . . one myself, but . . . but . . . but . . . but . . . but . . . (*Enrages, he shouts to the air.*) Klautus! Wherever you are, send Judas in! (*Wheels, in cold rage, to* JESUS.) Show *him* how you are determined!

(JUDAS *enters, terribly tense.*)

PILATE: (*Contemptuously.*) Judas. Can this be the man you follow?

JUDAS: This is . . . Jesus. Called the Christ.

PILATE: Very well. You tell him, Judas. Tell him what is waiting for him out there.

JUDAS: (*To* JESUS.) The world, Lord. The world. Everything you said has come true. I did not think that it was possible. Even Peter has denied you. As you predicted, three times, at the very door of your trial, he has denied. And he will not tell me if he did it to make all come true—or if he meant it. That's wrong of him, isn't it? He should tell me. You said it would all be made clear. Mustn't he tell me? Mustn't you? Mustn't someone? Please, only tell me. Haven't I at least that right, that I should know?

PILATE: (*Appalled.*) Judas. Judas.

JUDAS: (*Ignoring* PILATE.) And Caiaphas. Caiaphas held me back and gave me money, he had it all ready and counted out, the price of a slave, as you predicted, and he thanked me. He *thanked* me!

PILATE: (*Concerned.*) Judas.

JUDAS: And I threw it back at him, the bag broke, the money clanged all over the floor! And he only looked at me and smiled, smiled, smiled! As if he knew what I was going to do!

PILATE: (*Really worried about* JUDAS.) Judas . . .

JUDAS: (*To* JESUS.) You threw the money out of the temple. I threw the money back in! Does that mean something? Does that fulfill a prophecy? What have you involved me in?

PILATE: Judas, stop this!

JUDAS: (*To* JESUS.) Because I never meant for a moment to betray you. You know that. But, if it is all to come true, then I must, mustn't I? Mustn't I? But if I do, then I have fulfilled your prophecy. And if I have fulfilled your prophecy, then I haven't betrayed you. Or have I? Have I? Is that—is this—all that you wanted me for?

PILATE: Jesus, see what you reduce them to? Speak, help him. Tell him. Not me. I will leave him with you. Shall I leave you?

JUDAS: All has been made clear. All has been made clear. I am so many things at once. (*To* PILATE.) I am a loyal Roman, according to you. I am a loyal Jew, according to Caiaphas. (*Indicates* JESUS.) I am a loyal Christian, according to him. So why do I feel that I am betraying you all?

PILATE: Judas, you are descending into an animal state!

JUDAS: What animal state? Rome?

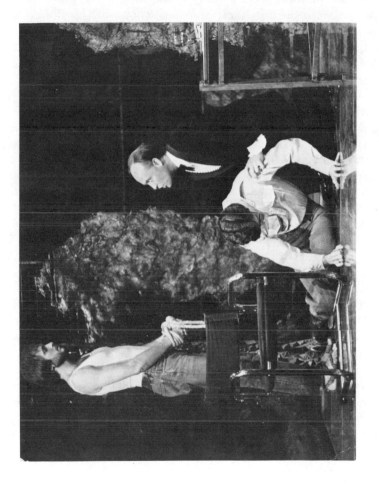

David Williams (JESUS), *Mark Harelik* (JUDAS), *and Laird Williamson* (PILATE) *in the PCPA production.*

PILATE: Judas. Go away. Rest yourself. (JUDAS *starts to leave.*
PILATE *stops him.*) No. Wait. Jesus. There is an alternative.
State your unpolitical nature, and . . . I will build you a temple of
your own, where you can teach as you will. As a scholar of your
faith, which you most certainly have had to be to pull this off, you
can lead these people in a way they will be led. You may create
the new religion that Rome needs, as Rome realizes that men
must have religion, even the best men. Be, not the head, but the
heart of Rome. These people care for nothing but prophecies
and rituals, the surface of religion. You can make that surface
work for them.

JUDAS: Yes, and for Rome, too. Say yes, Jesus, say yes.

PILATE: Once you are free this becomes a matter of civil law. They
will kill you.

JUDAS: That was the prophecy.

PILATE: I am bound by that law.

JUDAS: And by that prophecy.

PILATE: (*Looks from* JESUS *to* JUDAS, *back, erupts.*) One last plea!
Jesus, if you do this thing, you will be setting an example of
saintly self-sacrifice. Your followers will follow you, but what
they will follow is your example. They will die for a way of life,
they will fight for peace, they will kill for unity. The best will be
sacrificed to the worst for however long your name lasts. The
bright, the passionate, the passionately moral, the likes of Judas,
will follow you indeed, every step of your way. Sacrifice your
sacrifice. Fail yourself. Defeat me. But give Judas what he most
needs. (*Pause.* PILATE, *face to face with* JESUS, *kneels.*) You have
the Roman governor kneeling before you, Jesus!

JESUS: (*To heaven first, slowly to* JUDAS.) Our father who art in
heaven . . .

JUDAS: (*To himself first, slowly to* JESUS.) Yes, not here, no one
here.

JESUS: Hallowed be thy name.

JUDAS: Which we can never know.

JESUS: Thy kingdom come.

JUDAS: It is here in us.

JESUS: Thy will be done.

JUDAS: We are doing it. The deaths, the betrayals, the pains, they
have a purpose!

JESUS: On earth as it is in heaven.

JUDAS: Yes, without thought, without quarrels, as the stars move,
yes, yes, yes!

JESUS: Give us this day our daily bread . . .

JUDAS: If he does, we know he wants us to live, yes!

JESUS: And forgive us our trespasses as we forgive those who trespass against us.

JUDAS: If he punishes us then we know we have done wrong, yes!

JESUS: And lead us not into temptation . . .

JUDAS: He can't; everything that happens is his will. (PILATE *is backing away from this—to him—hideous antiphony.*)

JESUS: But deliver us from evil . . .

JUDAS: If he is all, then there is no evil . . .

JESUS: For thine is the kingdom . . .

JUDAS: No man can rule it!

JESUS: And the power . . .

JUDAS: No man deserves it!

JESUS: And the glory . . .

JUDAS: No man can bear it!

JESUS: Forever . . .

JUDAS: Forever!

JESUS: And ever . . .

JUDAS: And ever!

JESUS: Amen.

JUDAS: Amen, so be it, so be it, amen,amen!

PILATE: (*At the door.*) Klautus!

KLAUTUS: (*Enters immediately.*) Yes sir.

PILATE: Get them out of this office! Get him out of this office! Drain this sewage from my tower! Open the doors! Set him free! He is a free man! He is an intelligent disease!

KLAUTUS: (*Moves to* JESUS.) Yes sir.

PILATE: Have the soldiers whip him on the steps! See if that will satisfy the people. But get him out. Get him out of this tower! Unbind him! Relieve my presence of this suffering mud! (*As* KLAUTUS *unbinds* JESUS.) Judas, go. Or stay, as you choose. I will not pretend to give you orders. Come tomorrow if you will. At the usual time. Nothing has changed. Or stay and talk tonight . . .

JUDAS: (*Takes up* JESUS' *rope.*) I will follow him. Your prophecy is true, too. I will follow him. (JUDAS, JESUS *and* KLAUTUS *exit.* PILATE *is alone for a moment.* KLAUTUS *enters, timidly.*)

PILATE: There is water here to wash my hands? (KLAUTUS *pours water over* PILATE's *hands, hands* PILATE *a napkin to dry them.*) The savage was filthy—as usual. (KLAUTUS *removes the refreshments, keeping a concerned eye on* PILATE *as he does.*)

KLAUTUS: (*As he works.*) Sir?

PILATE: What is it, Klautus?

KLAUTUS: May I go now, sir?

PILATE: What? Oh, yes, of course, of course. Want to go and watch the suicide?

KLAUTUS: Suicide, sir?

PILATE: You want to go and watch Jesus' crucifixion?

KLAUTUS: (*Relieved.*) Oh, then it was *him* you meant to have crucified. I thought you meant me.

PILATE: You? What on earth for?

KLAUTUS: I listened, sir.

PILATE: Ah. And did you understand.

KLAUTUS: Not much, sir. He refused everything?

PILATE: He said nothing—to me.

KLAUTUS: Oh. I thought he might have whispered something.

PILATE: He'll be screaming something pretty soon. You can go out and hear that if you want to.

KLAUTUS: Out there? No, sir. I don't want to be out there among those people.

PILATE: They are our people, Klautus.

KLAUTUS: (*Finished with his work.*) Our people, sir? They aren't even . . . Their kings are slaves, and they sell us their people for slaves. Their priests say they take care of the people, but you had to break into their temple for gold when you needed money to build the people an aqueduct. They pretend to be proud of their race, but the service in the shops is slow because the old don't trust the young enough to hire them. It takes a religious holiday to get them to clean their city once a year. And their boys and girls sell themselves to our soldiers in the streets. Our people!

PILATE: And yet they had an empire once, with kings and armies and tribute from Egypt, too.

KLAUTUS: Not them, sir. That was a thousand years ago.

PILATE: Six hundred.

KLAUTUS: These people couldn't hold an empire together. They killed John and they'll kill Jesus, too, won't they?

PILATE: But we kill people, Klautus—often.

KLAUTUS: Only those who fight against the order. Sir.

PILATE: You are very fond of our "order, sir," aren't you?

KLAUTUS: Sir, any doubts I ever had about it—not that I ever had any . . .

PILATE: Of course not, of course not.

KLAUTUS: I mean, I feel free to talk to you, sir, because I've heard you say things—well—analyzing Rome.

PILATE: I do not criticize Rome, Klautus.

KLAUTUS: Oh, no, sir, of course not, why would you? I understand exactly what you've been doing all along. All those things I heard you say? Like that Rome is a lie, or there are no gods, or that you wanted to help destroy Rome? I realize now what you were doing. You were testing Judas, testing Jesus, testing me. You were giving them rope, stringing them along, giving them every possible chance. And now you've caught them, you've got them where you want them. (*Produces letter from pocket.*) Look, I've already written a letter to my father, telling him I was completely wrong to suspect you. (PILATE *takes letter, reads it.*) I know you want a Roman world, like you said to Jesus, I know that's the part you meant, you know exactly what you're doing. I just meant that, if I ever *had* been stupid enough to have any doubts about Rome exactly as it is, or to feel sentimental about any of these savage cannibals, well—what I've seen here, what I've learned from you, has completely convinced me how very fortunate we are to be Romans under Caesar!

PILATE: (*Automatically.*) Hail, Caesar.

KLAUTUS: (*Passionately.*) Hail, Caesar! (*He does a military turn and marches to the pedestal with Tiberius's bust, and is about to sacrifice, then turns and faces* PILATE.) Sir, won't you join me? (PILATE *lays* KLAUTUS's *letter down on his desk and very, very slowly walks to the pedestal. He starts to reach for salt, hesitates, and speaks.*)

PILATE: And if—I ask this hypothetically, Klautus—if Caesar were to be followed by an evil or an ignorant man . . . ?

KLAUTUS: Why, I would fight to restore the order, sir.

PILATE: But you would always be a Roman?

KLAUTUS: Yes sir!

PILATE: And if the slaves revolt?

KLAUTUS: I would put them down, sir.

PILATE: But we hope someday to rule without slaves, Klautus.

KLAUTUS: (*Blankly.*) Oh, I see, sir.

PILATE: We hope to take in all conquered people as citizens.

KLAUTUS: Ah, yes.

PILATE: We hope to bring our order to the entire world.

KLAUTUS: Yes, sir.

PILATE: Do you know why that is such hard work?

KLAUTUS: No sir.

PILATE: Out there in the great world are a million little worlds. They are in the heads of every little person. And in each one is a dream. Each one different. Dream of all the differences, there are more. And it is a single dream, really, that we wish to bring to the world, a dream of order.

KLAUTUS: You don't mean dreams like when you're asleep, sir?

PILATE: Those who dream so in their sleep are blessed.

KLAUTUS: Blessed by whom, sir?

PILATE: By whoever blesses. But while we dream this dream of perfect order, we set up temporary rules to live by. That's all they're meant to be, little expedient structures. But people so love order, so fear chaos, that they take our little temporary tents and turn them into temples. Laws, religions, whatever they're born into, become very dear to these people . . .

KLAUTUS: As order is to you, sir?

PILATE: (*In serious, sublime self-examination.*) Yes, as order is to me. And if change comes, these people are unhappy. But there is one thing they are always happy with, the dream inside their heads. There they are king or queen or princess or prince; they are adored, they are revenged, all is as they would have it be. But that is different for everyone, young or old, clumsy or wonderful, Roman, Jew, Christian or whatever, each has his world, and each tries to make the outside world conform, and the worlds in the heads of others conform, to his dream's royal command . . .

KLAUTUS: (*Thinks he's got it.*) I know what you mean, sir. Publius, your second aide, was champion in hurdles at the Academy. So he's always telling the ladies of the court that hurdling is the greatest sport, and all of that.

PILATE: (*Laughs, relaxes.*) Yes, yes, that is what I meant.

KLAUTUS: And he's always having the servants set up hurdle courses and challenging the rest of us to race.

PILATE: Yes, yes, I've heard the racket.

KLAUTUS: But I was first in archery, so I have had the courtyards rolled too hard for racing, and an archery range set up, because I always win from all of them at that.

PILATE: (*Patient, amused.*) I am sure you do.

KLAUTUS: And there's no dust flying at archery, so the ladies can come much closer.

PILATE: I see.

KLAUTUS: What's more, the Lady Jeniella has decided she wants to learn archery, which, of course, allows a fellow any number of opportunities for... (*Demonstrates circling a girl with his arm. Blushes.*) Well... you get my meaning, sir.

PILATE: I do.

KLAUTUS: So Publius is furious.

PILATE: (*Starts away.*) I will sleep now.

KLAUTUS: Or is this more what you mean, sir? The lady Rosabella is, well, as you know, hardly slim, and none of the other young noblemen here in the palace pay her any attention at all, so I tell her that she is slim and lovely and she'll let me have... just about... well...

PILATE: (*After a pause.*) Do you think Rosabella is treated fairly?

KLAUTUS: Well, none of the others even talk to her.

PILATE: And Publius?

KLAUTUS: Sir, he'd do it to me.

MARY: (*Enters below, at the foot of the cross.*) Oh, my God, my God, my son, my boy, I've murdered him. Oh, forgive me, God, I didn't know!

PILATE: Hail, Caesar! (*Sprinkles salt.*)

PETER: (*Enters to* MARY.) No, no, no, you haven't. You haven't done anything wrong. None of us has done anything wrong!

KLAUTUS: (*Sprinkles salt.*) Hail, Caesar.

PETER: We were, all of us, only allowed to help him in his glorious plan!

PILATE: Klautus, when someone asks you what you are, what do you say?

KLAUTUS: Sir?

MARY: Help him?

PETER: Yes. But you knew that. You always knew that.

MARY: I knew—I thought I knew that he had a glorious destiny.

PETER: More glorious than any of us could know.

PILATE: What do you say when someone asks you what you are?
KLAUTUS: Oh, well, of course I say that I am first assistant to Pontius Pilate, by proclamation of Tiberius...
PILATE: No, deeper than that.

PETER: Except you, of course. You knew. You always knew.

KLAUTUS: Well, I am the son of the senator and tribune, Marcellus...
PILATE: Deeper than that.

PETER: You know you always knew.

KLAUTUS: Well... I am a young man.
PILATE: Deeper.
KLAUTUS: Well...

PETER: Come away with us. Our work here is done. The others are waiting for us. Come and help us through this time of sorrow. (*Begins to draw* MARY *away.*)

KLAUTUS: Oh, I see. Yes sir. You're testing me again. Well, yes, sir. Of course. I am a Roman.

PETER: Come tell us what you know you always knew.
MARY: Well, yes, of course, I always knew... something.

PILATE: And if someone were to say to you, "Here, here is a way where no one is mistreated or subjugated, a world where men need not plot or sacrifice or watch their words or kowtow to Pontius Pilate ever again?"

PETER: Of course you knew.

KLAUTUS: Well, sir, that would be—except that it would always be an honor to work with you, sir—that would be a much better world, of course.

PETER: You know you always knew.

PILATE: And if to have that world you had to renounce Rome?

KLAUTUS: I see. You're not going to get me to say anything wrong, sir. I would choose Rome.

> MARY: Of course I did. Yes, yes, of course I did. I always knew that he had a glorious destiny. Why, even at his birth, the angels sang. (MARY *and* PETER *exit.*)

PILATE: You are a Roman?
KLAUTUS: Yes sir.
PILATE: The best product of Rome?
KLAUTUS: That is not for me to say, sir.
PILATE: Always and eternally a Roman?
KLAUTUS: Yes sir.
PILATE: Right or wrong, a Roman?
KLAUTUS: Yes sir.
PILATE: In life or death?
KLAUTUS: Yes.
PILATE: Peace or war?
KLAUTUS: Yes.
PILATE: You *believe* in Rome?
KLAUTUS: Yes *sir!*
PILATE: Barbarian!
KLAUTUS: What?
PILATE: Barbarian!
KLAUTUS: Sir?
PILATE: Barbarian! Leave me to my sleep!
KLAUTUS: Sir, I . . .
PILATE: (*Slaps* KLAUTUS.) Out of my sight! Barbarian! Barbarian! Barbarian! (PILATE *stalks off to his bedchamber.* KLAUTUS *stands, angry and stunned. Turns to go, sees his letter on* PILATE's *desk, picks it up, slowly and deliberately tears it into scraps, exits, grinning.*)

CURTAIN

The Bathtub
Lisa Shipley

The Bathtub was first performed by The Womyn's Theatre in Seattle, Washington, as part of the New Women Playwrights Festival. The production opened on March 19, 1979, with the following cast:

JOYCE	Roberta Levitow
LEANN	Nancy Houfek

Directed by Susan Richardson-Glass

Photo by Michael Drew.

The Bathtub
Lisa Shipley

JOYCE *is sitting in the bathtub. A small black tray fits over its edges and is covered with small clay creatures that she is busily modeling.* LEANN *is sitting on the toilet doing a crossword puzzle.*

LEANN: 19 down, caused St. Vitus' Dance, four letters.

JOYCE: Mold.

LEANN: (*Writing.*) Yeah, that fits. 24 across, four letters.

JOYCE: (*Smashes clay animal in frustration.*) Shit!

LEANN: (*Looks up.*) What's wrong this time? Put a head on backwards?

JOYCE: I'm not getting anywhere with my work today. (*The phone rings.* LEANN *picks it up and holds it next to* JOYCE's *ear, continues to do crossword puzzle.*) Hello? Larry? Hello. I'm all right, mostly. What? Of course I'm still in the bathtub. I told you that until . . . Have you been talking with my mother? Yes, yes, I don't dry my hair in the tub anymore. I know, it even says not to right on the dryer. So is *that* why you called, so that I'd get electrocuted, die right here on the phone while we're talking? Larry, you *can't* get electrocuted talking on the telephone. Don't you even go to old movies anymore? Audrey Hepburn never got electrocuted talking on the phone in the bathtub . . . Well, I'm sorry you don't go out much anymore, Larry. I really don't think that's my fault . . . I can't help it if *you* do . . . Why do you want to know? (*Looks at* LEANN.) You'd be threatened either way. Look, Larry, I don't want to talk about it and I'd appreciate it if you wouldn't call my mother. I'm not doing very well today and . . . Goodbye Larry . . . All right . . . Okay, goodb— . . . I don't want your . . . He hung up.

LEANN: (*Hangs up phone, looks at* JOYCE *who has slumped back into the tub, continues doing her crossword puzzle. Silence.*) What's a seven-letter word meaning mental anguish?

JOYCE: (*Counting.*) H-U-S-B-A-N . . .

LEANN: It has to start with an "A" . . . a-n-x-i-e-t-y.

JOYCE: (*Looks at* LEANN, *then begins aggressively kneading the clay.*) Well, don't you want to know what he said?

LEANN: Of course.

JOYCE: Then why didn't you ask me?

LEANN: We have a contract not to pry.

JOYCE: Sometimes it would be easier if you'd just ask me first. Without me having to tell you first.

LEANN: Okay, okay. What did Larry say?

JOYCE: Oh, nothing. Just the usual.

LEANN: (*Sighs, returns to her puzzle.*) What's a twelve-letter word meaning "formerly of Mesopotamian stock?"

JOYCE: Why do you always avoid talking about my ex-husband?

LEANN: Look Joyce, I asked you what he said and all you did was give a smartass answer.

JOYCE: He wants to know why I'm still in the tub and when I'm going to come out.

LEANN: So does everyone else.

JOYCE: He's been calling my mother and telling her things.

LEANN: That doesn't surprise me.

JOYCE: Is that all you can say, "That doesn't surprise me?" Why not say, "What things?" Why am I always the one who has to bring up the issues?

LEANN: What issues?

JOYCE: Like how you avoid bringing up issues.

LEANN: You're getting to be real exhausting, you know that? You know what's wrong with you really? Something bad is happening to your bodily fluids because you're in the bathtub all the time. You're losing essential salts and it's ruining your sense of humor.

JOYCE: Now you're making fun of me.

LEANN: Maybe I should just leave the room for a while.

JOYCE: Oh great, just walk out and leave me here. That's a hell of an adult way to have an argument.

LEANN: And you're the example of adult behavior? Why, if you ran any farther away you'd be down the drain right now.

JOYCE: Is that supposed to be funny?

LEANN: Joyce, I'm losing my patience. You've been in this bathtub for two weeks now, and I've tried to understand. I've read you books, brought you coffee, combed your hair, played Scrabble and now I'm reduced to doing crossword puzzles that I detest because *you* won't get out of the bathtub, demand my company and are obsessed with these little clay dolls.

JOYCE: I am not obsessed and they are not dolls.

LEANN: I'm going out for a while, all right? I'll be back later and fix us something to eat, all right? Spaghetti or something?

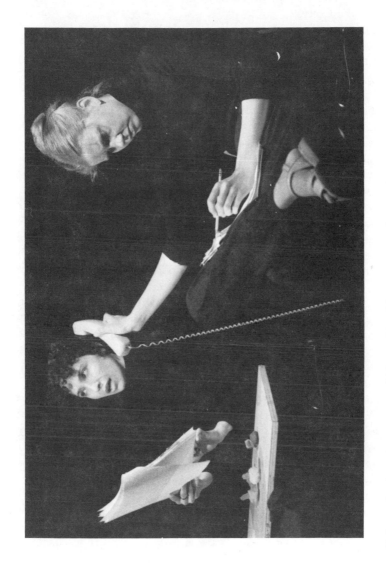

Roberta Levitow (JOYCE) and Nancy Houfek (LEANN) rehearse the Womyn's Theatre production.

JOYCE: (*Pouting.*) You know what really bothers me? When I left
Larry, I said to myself, I'm never going to get involved with
anyone like him again. But you know what? Sometimes you're
just like Larry.

LEANN: And sometimes you're just like my goddamned mother!
(*She grabs the door, fumbles with it, curses.*)

JOYCE: Wait a minute, you just can't (LEANN *exits, slamming door.*)
say something like that and walk out. Come back here. Leann!
Hey Leann! I just can't believe it. An argument in the bathtub.
Things *are* taking a turn for the worse. Now what do I do? She
violated my sanctuary, my safe place, my cure for depression,
fatigue, hunger. Arguments, banishments, everything. (*Yells.*)
Leann, are you still there? (*Silence.*) I was going to tell you about
my first sexual experience in a bathtub. (*Silence.*) I guess I'll just
have to tell you later. (*During the next speech, she plays with the
clay figures, talks to herself, and yells as if talking to* LEANN.) For
fourteen days and fourteen nights it rained down upon them, she
was commanded to build an ark. In her tub she survived while
the rest of the world perished in the deluge. Hey Leann, it's not
what you might think. The sexual experience. My stepfather was
standing in the shower. Leann? All right, don't listen. My tub's
enough, anyway. It is enough and I knew it would be, hot water,
a few artifacts, an ebony tray to set them on. My cousins had an
ebony tray just like this one ... my sexy cousins. They had an
ebony tray covered with lotions and exotic beauty devices, most
of which were bright red. They were so gorgeous and sexy.
(*Loudly.*) Did your cousins have ebony trays too? (*Silence.*)
Listen, I really want to tell you about my stepfather and the
shower. I was six and I walked into the bathroom. He was
standing there in a cloud of steam, his arms stretched above his
head, reaching for the shower spray. He shouted, "Get the hell
out of here," and then there was this black hole between his
knees and his stomach. When I remember this picture I still see a
big black hole. I never took a shower from that day on, even in
gym, can you imagine? I hate showers. (*Pause.*) Maybe we could
get a bathtub big enough for both of us, what do you say?
(*Silence.*) I'm floating and I feel a little helpless. I just remembered the craziest thing! When I was twelve I almost totally lost
my passion for bathing. You know, when I broke my leg? It was
in a cast for months and months. When they took the cast off my
leg was mostly dead skin. It also made me wretched to think my

leg was rotting all the while and I didn't even know it, like I should have been able to prevent it. They put me right into the tub, my first immersion in months, and the dead skin slowly floated off my leg and stayed on the surface of the water, floating there like a bunch of lotus with leprosy. Yuk! What do you think of that? I'm starting to get real depressed in this bathtub. I say (*Shouts.*) I'm starting to get real depressed in this goddamned bathtub! (*The phone rings and she ignores it.*) Don't bother, it's probably just goddamned Larry. Romans died in their tubs, did you know that? A sensualist's hara-kiri. SSST . . . a small cut at the wrist and then eternal watery bliss, not at all like drowning. A little wine in a winecolored tub. She wouldn't like to hear me talking like that. She doesn't suffer from heroic self-doubts. (*Yells.*) Leann, why don't you suffer from heroic self-doubts? (*Silence.*) I know I know, I admit it, I have exhausted all this tub's possibilities. It hasn't at all been like birth or rebirth, meditation or amniotic fluids. I'm just slowly deteriorating. Soon I'll be covered with barnacles, or beached, a ship . . . like "she" ships. The sea is a woman and ships are a woman. Eve left him holding the bag on shore and evermore were ships and seas for woman named. I cast off casting about. I'm floating and I feel a little helpless. I'm getting smaller and smaller, I'm the incredible shrinking woman. I'm getting too lonely Leann. Come back in, we can play cards again. (*Silence.*) What are we going to have for dinner? It's like I said, I can't help it if there isn't a stove in here. I am *not* trying to avoid responsibility! Please don't bring any more chili in here. You know why.

LEANN: (*Knocks, talks through door.*) Joyce, I want you to get out of the tub.

JOYCE: Why?

LEANN: (*Off.*) Because I don't want to eat my spaghetti alone. I need someone on the other end to suck up the pasta. You know, we each suck an end of the pasta and bump noses. Won't that be fun? More fun than playing with your dolls?

JOYCE: Don't ask me to get out of the tub.

LEANN: (*Off.*) Take your goddamned thumb out of your mouth!

JOYCE: What's so goddamned wrong with spending a little time in the bathtub?

LEANN: (*Off.*) You've been in there for two weeks!

JOYCE: I have? Two weeks? Only two weeks? (*Panics.*) It's not nearly long enough. Go away! Almost lost sense of time . . . but I need another month, to lose all sense of time, at least one more month.

LEANN: (*Off.*) Right now you have ten minutes to come to dinner.

JOYCE: Ten minutes! A lifetime? You make it sound so simple. "Joyce, get out of the bathtub." Do you know how many years it took me to get this far? To actually arrive at the bathtub? Eons! Centuries!

LEANN: (*Off.*) History is over! Wake up!

JOYCE: I can't leave my sanctuary for a plate of spaghetti.

LEANN: (*Off.*) Then leave it for me. I want you to come have dinner with me.

JOYCE: I can't yet. Look, it's not just the water, although god knows it's wonderful enough. It's the ebony tray, the animals . . .

LEANN: (*Off.*) Think about giving up bathing altogether, like all *addicts* eventually have to.

JOYCE: I'm not an addict! Give up my bath? How could you suggest such a thing!

LEANN: (*Off.*) Easy, my spaghetti's getting cold and I think you have an unhealthy relationship with your bathtub.

JOYCE: That's what my mother says about us.

LEANN: (*Off.*) Yes, but she thought your relationship with Larry was healthy, so what does she know?

JOYCE: Don't be a smartass.

LEANN: (*Off.*) I'm not a smartass, I'm fucking angry. I'm exhausted too, so why don't you get the motherfuck out of the tub!

JOYCE: (*Working herself into a rage.*) I don't ever want to get out of this tub, ever. I'm exhausted too, I'm fucking tired too! Of everything. I don't want anything, no time, no routines, just warm water, amoeba water, one-celled animal seawater. I want to make little clay animals. I don't want to participate! I want to make little clay animals and move them around on my ebony tray. I want to think about everything that ever happened to me in a bathtub and every circumstance that drove me crying into the bathtub, every private moment in here, each one laid side by side. Why the hell did I bother to get the hell out all those other times? Someone is always screaming for you to get out of the tub! It took all this time to say no, NO! Noooooooo! (*She starts flinging the animals around the room, then the tray. She slumps back into the water, exhausted.*)

LEANN: (*Off.*) What's going on in there? (*Silence.*) Joyce? (*Silence.*)

JOYCE: I'm stroking my breasts. I'm touching my body all over, everywhere. That's all I want, to touch my own body. (*Silence.* LEANN *stands silently outside the door.*) Leann? Are you there? (*Silence. Yells.*) Hey, Leann, come back here. Leann? (*Pause.*) I guess I really freaked her out this time. (*Looks at hand.*) I'm beginning to resemble an albino prune. (*Restless.*) Leann? What am I going to do? I lose face either way, especially if I *don't* get out. I wonder if I really could rot entirely away? (*Lies back in tub.*)

LEANN: (*Off.*) Are you done touching your body all over?

JOYCE: (*Surprised she's there.*) Yes! I mean, no, not quite.

LEANN: Well, when you're done touching your breasts, you could touch mine. After all, they're just like your own. (*Pause.*)

JOYCE: Yours are bigger, bigger and rounder. Mine are like miniature hydrogen bombs and they are located lower down on my torso. (*Silence.*) You could come stroke *my* breasts.

LEANN: I can't. The door's locked. (*Pause.*)

JOYCE: So I have to get out of the tub?

LEANN: Either that or I call the landlord. (*Silence.*)

JOYCE: I'll get nosebleed if I stand up. (*She starts to rise slowly.*) Leann, will you bring me a towel?

LEANN: Can you open the door?

JOYCE *stands up. Of course, she is naked and dripping wet. She stands shivering for a while, then opens the door. They stare at each other for a while, then* LEANN *covers her with a towel.*

JOYCE: How come the door was locked?

LEANN: I locked it before I left.

JOYCE: Did you trick me?

LEANN: (*Hesitates.*) I don't know.

THE END

Imitations
Nancy Larson

Imitations was first performed at the Padua Hills Writers Conference in Los Angeles. The production opened in July, 1978, and was performed by Bob Glaudini under the author's direction.

In 1978 it was also produced by the British Film Institute in London, the Midlands, Cardiff, and Edinburgh, again performed by Mr. Glaudini.

Photo by James Marzullo.

Imitations
Nancy Larson

A DERELICT *enters the playing area carrying a dirty plastic shopping bag filled to overflowing with junk. He lets the bag fall to the ground. He drops to his hands and knees and sniffs the area like a bloodhound.*

DERELICT: (*Angry.*) Somebody's been here all right. Don't try to tell me any different now. That would only make me mad 'cause then I'd know *for sure* that you was one of them pack of liars out there... Don't even talk to me about liars, I hate them so much!

(*He takes a banged-up old water pistol out of his pants pocket, puts it to his crotch, lifts his leg and starts squirting water like a dog staking his territory. As he does this, he growls.*) Grrr... Grrr... Grrr... Ruff! Ruff! Ruff! (*Puts gun back into his pants pocket.*) If you get what I mean... and just in case you don't... (*He takes a ratty whisk broom from his bag, and uses the stick end to draw a semi-circle around the playing area in front of the audience. We realize that he is near to tears.*)

I'm gonna spell it out for you. (*Puts broom back in bag.*) Don't nobody cross that there line! Okay? We got that straight? Good... Hey, hey, listen now. I got no personal gripe with you. All you gotta do is to just understand that this is my home, that's all. I mean, you wouldn't want me traipsing through your home, now would you? I should certainly say not! I know this place like the back of my hand, to put it very mildly. Like, for instance, bet you didn't know there used to be cobweb right exactly there. (*He points out the location by squirting his pistol at a crevice in a boulder.*) That was in A OK condition when I left here this morning. Some guy stepped right on it with his fat hiking boots. Footprint's right here if you don't believe me. (*Bends to sniff the ground and makes a face.*) You can still smell the rubber. That was somebody's home he stepped on! What the heck did he care? And you shoulda seen the delicious dinner that spider had waiting for him, too. Some people ... Some people. Where does God find people like that? You know, I'm not always like this. I mean, I'm usually a nice guy. Ask anybody. It's just that... It's just that... Well, if you *must* know (*Takes a deep breath.*), I once kinda liked this girl, but she got in an accident last night. She passed away with her panties twisted down around her ankles. (*He shivers.*) Gives me the creeps just to think about it. I thought you oughta know that right off the bat so's you won't get all bent outta shape later on. Anyway, she had these gigantic blue eyes that made you feel that you were swimming. I mean drowning. Oh yeah, also, she wore pearls in her ears.

Hey, that reminds me . . . I know it's in here somewhere. (*He digs in his pocket, turning it inside out to carefully retrieve a "diamond."*) 'Cause I put it there myself. (*Holds the "diamond" up for inspection.*) I *was* saving this for a special occasion. (*He sighs.*) Know what it is? Yes sirree Bob. A genuine diamond. Old eagle eyes, that's me, found it right exactly here in the dirt. (*Takes out his pistol and squirts the spot.*) Right there. Know how I know the real McCoy? 'Cause for a whole week I showed it to every person that I saw, and do you know that not one single one of them said that it wasn't, 'cept that squirt kid, but kids don't count anyways. I was going to give it to her.

(*He sits down to ponder the situation, staring at the "diamond." Angry.*) So, now what am I supposed to do? Huh? Do *I* leave *my* diamonds any old which way on the ground? Great. That's all I need. Another burden. Let the world die for my sins. See if I care, leaving their diamonds strewn every old which way . . . Boy, I'm telling you, those pearls in her ears made me so hungry. (*He tosses the diamond into his mouth and swallows it.*) HEY! (*He jumps to his feet and pulls up his sleeve to check his nonexistent watch.*) Oh boy oh boy oh boy oh boy.

(*He takes out a greasy McDonald's sack from his bag and swings it from his thumb and index finger.*) It's lunch time . . . First we take out the old tablecloth. (*He sets the sack aside and takes a ratty plastic floral tablecloth from the bag. He spreads it on the ground, taking great care to smooth the edges.*) Don't think I'm just doing this 'cause you're here. Oh no. I like to do things right too, you know. (*He takes half-eaten burritos and hamburgers out of the sack and puts them to one side. Next he takes out a number of french fries and ritualistically arranges them in a neat row.*)

She loved french fries. She could really make a pig out of herself over them things. (*He takes a limp fry and dramatically crosses himself with it. Then he pops it into his mouth. In quick succession, he does the same with all but two of the fries. He begins to eat the burrito and hamburger morsels.*) Mmm mmm mmmm. I'd invite you to dig in with me but as you can see, there's only enough for me and the temple. (*He gobbles up his food, speaking with his mouth full.*)

If a body knows where to hunt, then there's no good reason in the world why he can't eat like a king. Here. I'm gonna show you something. (*He stands to walk to a small boulder which he rolls over to uncover a hole.*) It's a secret... (*He lovingly picks up a burlap bag from the hole.*)

This is the Holy Sacred Bag. (*He kisses it and walks to the edge of the stage. He kneels, facing audience, and gently empties the contents on the ground. Out tumble sizable pieces of broken colored glass from bottles. He piles the pieces into a pile as he talks.*) This is going to be, when I finish, the Holy Sacred Rattlesnake and Mosquito Temple. Used to be here all the time, but people would kick it and step on it and what not unless I was here to guard it. So now, whenever I'm here, it's here, and whenever I'm not, it's not. Like magic. Anyway, you might be wondering just what in the heck a Holy Sacred Rattlesnake and Mosquito Temple is doing out here in the wilds. So, I'm gonna show you.

(*He takes the two remaining french fries to the Temple.*) The first thing you do is you take some food, in this case, two french fries, and you crumple it up good on top here, like this. (*He crumples the fries on top of the Temple.*) That's for the rattlesnakes, by the way. See, you gotta show them respect, 'cause snakes are creatures of the creator too. That way by the time they finish their meal, they don't feel so much like sliding over there to bite me. Get it? Just the same, it don't pay to overfeed them, 'cause they'd be expecting to get that much food all the time. And then you could find yourself in some real trouble, if you couldn't come up with the goods, I mean. (*He uses his hand to demonstrate a snake striking.*) SSST.

(*He takes a safety pin from the underside of his lapel.*) This is where my good old Ma used to keep her sewing needles. So don't say that I said that she never taught me nothing good!

(*He stabs himself in the finger with a grand theatrical gesture and squeezes blood on one of the top pieces of glass.*) And this is for the mosquitos, in case you didn't guess. Fact is, it's not really enough to feed all them buggers. But I think they're intelligent enough to know that it's the thought that counts. Did I just say what I think I just said? (*Disgusted.*) What a bunch of crapola. The thought that counts, who's kidding who there, buster! Aw forget it! (*He puts the pin back under his lapel.*)

Sometimes about this time I take a little schnoozaroo. And when I do (*He pulls a long scarf from his bag.*) I tie this around me like so.

(He lifts his various undergarments to tie it around his bare middle.)
Know why? It's so the devil can't get into me through my belly-
button when I'm asleep. It works pretty good too, most of the time.
(He pulls the scarf off of himself.) I don't have to do that now, 'cause
anyway, I can't sleep. My brain only wants to think about her.

   The first time I met her was when I'm taking my regular siesta
and I hear this click, click. *(Makes the sound with his tongue.)* My
eyes fly open 'cause I'm thinking that some kids is toying with the
temple stones. But no. It was her, crouched up in front of me. She
was taking my picture with a camera. I didn't know what to think. I
was kinda mad. What a thing to wake up to: click, click, click. My
brain musta shown through my eyes, 'cause she stopped. *(He giggles.)*
Her skirt had crept up way above her knees. *(Bragging.)* I had my
picture taken before, you know. Sure I did. Just a few days before
that. And all because I just happened to be walking by Joe's
shoeshine parlor. He's this Negro man that always says something
nice to me. Like, "Hey, how ya do-in mah ma-an," or "Hey brodah,
how is it go-in." *(He thinks he's doing black talk.)* So I count on him
as being one of my bosom buddies, even though I kinda get in his
hair sometimes, at which time he may say something not so very
nice like, "What the hell boy, you back again? I ain't got no change
for you today." Then I walk away all hurt and lonesome and I don't
show up for a few days . . . He knows I don't just like him for his
money. Anyway, I know he's sorry 'cause when I do show up again
he treats me extra special nice.

   So, as I was saying, I'm making my usual visit to Joe's Shoe Shine
Parlor, shooting the crap with my buddy Joe, when this guy with
really dusty shoes plunks hisself in the chair for a shine. So Joe
starts going to it. *(Demonstrates, with sound effects.)* But pretty soon,
I start seeing something funny. The shinier this guy's shoes get, the
more you notice how dull his *eyes* are. Like the fog is rolling in. So
I'm thinking that this guy's making one big fat mistake to *ever* get
his shoes shined. And I try and tell him this, but my words get all
confused. Then Joe starts brushing me away like a fly, I mean a
mosquito. So I get some dirt from under the sidewalk palm and
dump it on one of the guy's shoes, so's Joe can see what it is that
I'm saying. Well, the guy don't appreciate this, to put it very mildly.
(He giggles.) You can tell that Joe is *really* mad at me. Know what he
does? He turns me around by the shoulders and steers me into this
photo booth next to the stand and he plops me down on the stool,
and tells me, "You wait there till I comes to fetch you!" Then he

slams closed the curtains like if it was a door, I'm sure it would have shook a whole city block.

(*Starts giggling again.*) Sitting there all by myself, I start to thinking it's pretty darn funny. I mean, if this guy had any sense at all he would *pay* me to dump dirt on his shoes, and I start laughing, my brains out over this, when, flash . . . flash, flash, flash! Joe musta put a quarter in the machine 'cause there I am getting my picture took. (*Puzzled.*) Or, did I dream that part? But this is not what I wanted to talk about . . . Who me? (*Pointing to himself, as if talking to an unseen person.*) What I wanted to talk about? . . . What? Okay. Okay. It's okay now. I remember. *So!* Here I was getting my picture took for the second time in a row! It turns out that she was a college student and had to take a lot of silly pictures and ask a lot of dumb questions to pass the grade.

Boy, let me tell you, have things changed. I once went to college, you know. Auto mechanics college. See, my Ma got hooked up to this guy who was all hotsy totsy to take her to greener pastures. He used words like that, hotsy totsy and greener pastures, so you can just imagine what kind of slick guy he was. But she wouldn't leave me till she knew that my future was secure. So she signed me up for this school. I guess she didn't think I could take good care of myself. Jeesh. (*Sighs.*) Well, pretty soon the two of them got ants in their pants and couldn't wait for me to finish. I might not have been the smartest kid in the class, but I sure as heck wasn't the dumbest either! I could have been a mechanic. But Bob, that's his name, Bob, he got me this job as an elevator boy, and off they went. (*Sarcastic.*) Thanks a lot Bob, old pal, old buddy. *For two whole years.* Going up, going down, going up, going down, day in, day out, rain or shine, going up, going down, going up, going down. Till one day those doors opened, and I hightailed it out of that elevator so fast you'd of thought a bolt of lightning hit me. That's all I remember. Next thing you know, here I am. (*Defensively.*) And here I'm gonna stay. 'Cause I like it here. And so did she.

She took so many pictures of this place, and of me, and of the stuff in my bag, and of me putting food on the temple, and she asked me every sort of question that you could imagine, and some even that you couldn't. Like, know what she asked me? She asked me where do I go to the bathroom. Now, isn't that a stupid question? You don't just go around asking people stuff like that. Would an intelligent person ask that? Would Johnny Carson ask somebody that? No! So I was really mad and I clammed right up. But then I got to thinking. If for instance, now, if just for instance a astronaut happened to walk up to me and say, "Go ahead buddy, ask me anything you want," well, I gotta admit, I'd sure want to ask him when he's in space or walking on the moon, "Where do you go to the bathroom?" So maybe, if you think of it in that way you could forgive her, which is what I ended up doing, 'specially since she brought me this five-course never-been-touched-before dinner from Jack-'n-the-Box.

Well, before you knew it, she was getting nicer and nicer. Jeeze, she practically lived here, 'cept at night, you know. (*Proudly.*) See this coat? (*Smells the torn coat he's wearing as one would smell a flower.*) She gave it to me, tied up in red ribbons and all. I got so choked up. Know what she said to me? "Can't let my best boyfriend freeze to death." She said that. Honest to God. My best boyfriend. (*He takes a mangled red ribbon from his breast pocket, puts it to his face and inhales deeply. He ties it to a nearby tree as he makes up this chant.*)

> Who spilt the milk? Who spilt the milk?
> No use prying, I says. Who spilt the milk?
> Who spilt the milk? No use dying, I says.
> Who spilt the milk? Who spilt the milk?
> No use crying.

(*He shoots the base of the tree with his pistol to water it. Then he shoots the pistol into his mouth to take a drink. He turns to the audience, as he puts away the gun.*)

So you can see why it wasn't long before she had me doing my imitations. Bet you didn't know I did imitations. That's cause I never used to do them for people, till she came along. Like, remember before when I said I could have been a mechanic? I got that from Marlon Brando when he said, (*Doing an impression.*) "I could have been a champ, (*Beat.*) Stella." Or how 'bout this? (*He does Ed Sullivan and Donald Duck or whatever.*) And before I knew it I was doing my Fred imitation. (*He can't dance, but you can tell that he really thinks he can, doing all sorts of fancy gyrations. He sings off-key as he dances.*)

> I'm singin' in the rain—splash splash,
> Just singin' in the rain—splash splash,
> What a glorious feelin',
> I'm hap-hap-happy again—splash splash . . .

(*He stops to catch his breath.*) I really can relate to that song 'cause I really *do* like to sing in the rain. Most people don't. They like to

Bob Glaudini (DERELICT) *in the Padua Hills Writers Conference production.*

run out of the rain. I guess they don't like things falling on them.
(*He realizes that he stepped on some remaining food and messed up his
tablecloth while dancing.*) Holy smokes, what a mess. And how. (*He
shakes out the cloth and puts it back in his bag. Regards the ground.*)
Oh oh. Crumbs. Crumby crumbs. (*He takes the whisk broom from the
bag and sweeps the area.*) I'm gonna turn you over my knee and
spank you good, making messy all over my house. (*He repeatedly
and violently whacks the dirt with the broom.*) Hey! Remember what
the Indians used to do to cover up their tracks? (*He demonstrates,
brushing away his tracks from behind.*) I really admire that. (*He puts
the broom away.*)

Hey, don't make any mistakes, 'cause she wasn't all perfect and
sweet. I wouldn't want you to think that, oh no. She was darn good
at saying some pretty depressing things at times. Like telling me
that sooner or later they wouldn't let me live here any more and
that I'd have to start making plans for my future and what not. (*He
puts his hands to his ears, elbows out.*) I'm not listening to you. No
I'm not. (*To drown out her voice.*) Do di do di do di dum dum di
dum! (*Drops his hands.*) Something like that could really ruin a
guy's day, believe you me. She could get me to feeling so sad that
I'd have to take out my one hundred percent guaranteed to cheer
me upper. If you want, I can show it to you. Got it right here in the
old baggaroo. (*He starts digging through his bag.*) I know it's somewhere in here 'cause I put it there myself. (*Still fishing through the
junk.*) You wouldn't believe the valuable items some people *choose*
to throw away. Makes me sick! I can't save it all, so I just save the
cream of the pie, so to speak. Here it is! (*He holds up a tattered comic
strip. Sheepishly.*) I guess it kind of got messed up. Lucky for you I
got it in the old brain. (*Stands up readying himself for a performance.*)

See, here's this regular guy called Ziggy. He's wearing glasses.
(*Uses his fingers to form the glasses.*) See? (*He has transformed himself
into a real schlemiel.*) And he's taking a regular walk. (*Does so.*) When
he comes upon a hippy freak who says to him . . . (*He turns himself
into a hippy freak by rounding his shoulders and messing up his hair.*)
"Hey man. The pigs could machine gun us down any time they
want to. (*Pretends to hold a machine gun.*) e-e-e-e-e-e!" (*Back to Ziggy
who jumps in fright.*) But Ziggy keeps walking along till this
preacher comes up to him and says, (*Ziggy changes into a blind
preacher, madly groping with an outstretched hand.*) "Repent . . . Repent brother. For the end of the world is coming!" (*Back to Ziggy, a
little bewildered.*) But Ziggy keeps right on walking. Maybe he

scratches his head a little (*Does so.*) like he's kinda confused, till he comes upon this scientist guy making a speech. (*As the scientist.*) "The way we are testing atomic energy, one accident and POOF! That's the end of us." (*As Ziggy.*) All of a sudden Ziggy tears off down the street. (*Does so.*) He runs into the nearest soda fountain all out of breath and screams at the guy, "Give me a triple hot fudge sundae with the works and make it quick!" Get it? "And make it quick!" (*He is in hysterics at his joke. Finally he wipes the tears from his eyes.*)

Anyway, know what she said when I showed that to her? That I was capable of profound thoughts. Just between you and me, I think that she wanted to kiss me on the lips 'cause she moved in real close to look into my eyes. But instead she said, "You think a lot, don't you?" Sure I think a lot. But in my mind I was thinking of feeling her up. (*He closes his eyes and feels the breasts of an imaginary girl. He starts to thrust his pelvis at her.*) Ooh ooh ooooooh, do you feel good. (*Feels at her crotch.*) Let me just . . . (*Grabs her ass and pulls her to him.*) Let me just . . . If there's a God then *please* let me just . . . (*Tries to "enter" her.*) Ooh Ooh Ooh now . . . (*His eyes fly open. He jumps up.*)

WHAT? Oh God no! WHAT? (*He throws himself to the ground and puts his ear to the earth, listening.*) Oh no. Uh uh. They ain't coming to get me yet. No sirree! (*Scared, he addresses the ground.*) You're not, are you? (*Puts his ear to the ground to listen again. He jumps up, defiantly brushing himself off.*) Because I have not yet made my future plans. Boy, do I need a cigarette. (*He goes to the audience with the air of a professional hustler.*) Hey buddy, got a cigarette? Got a light? (*Presumably the audience member is digging for a light.*)

While you're digging around in there, if you run across any spare change . . . Never mind. I'm only kidding about that part. Wouldn't want you to think that I was greedy. That's the last thing I want. Like I don't got enough problems. (*Lights his cigarette.*)

Hey, wait a minute. Don't go away. 'Cause I got something for you. And you're gonna like it. Or else. (*He runs to a secret hiding place to retrieve an apple. He spits and polishes it on the way back to the audience member. He thrusts it before the man's face.*) Here you go, partner. Go on. Take a bite. (*He makes a mischievous grimace as the man takes a bite. He grabs the apple back and returns it to the hiding place.*)

I *was* saving it for something special. You know, we had an apple tree in our back yard. Sometimes when my ma used to take me to the movies, she took along apples so's she wouldn't have to buy me candy. Jeez, that lady could be cheap. I remember her taking me to one movie starring Brigitte Bardot or Sophia Loren, anyway you know the type I mean. (*Indicates ample bosoms with cupped hands.*) In this one particular scene she was standing by this pond taking off her clothes. First she wriggles out of her skirt. (*He mimes, exaggerating her movements.*) Then she slides her sweater over her head. (*He does this, tossing the sweater aside, patting his hair back into place.*) Then she takes off her slip. (*Brings down the straps one by one and steps out of it.*) So there she is standing there in her panties and brassière when, guess what? A train comes by and blocks the view! Can you believe that? And by the time the train passes, she's in the pond and you can't see nothing 'cept her head. Boy, that made me mad. So the next day I sneak into the movie house and watch the movie over and over again. I keep hoping that train will be late just once. And each time the train goes by I get madder and madder until after the fifth time I go completely berserk. Next thing I know, I'm ripping the seats to shreds with my pocket knife. You can believe me when I say I got smacked good for that. Anyway, I was just a kid then.

So then *she* comes back day after day, taking her dumb pictures and asking her crumby questions. (*Softening.*) But I don't mind, 'cause when she's here my face changes. I mean it. Like I'm sure I wouldn't recognize myself if I walked into a mirror. I'd probably say, "Hey, who's that famous movie star," or something. But then she goes and asks me where my mother is.

This place is lousy with weirdos, you know. Don't think I'm kidding either. A gang of drunken kids could come in here and boing me on the head. You never know. Not that I give a crap about this smelly carcass. I just want you to know that I can't take responsibility for anybody here. Myself included. We got that straight? Good. That's what I said to her by way of changing the subject. But she don't forget that easy. And she asks me *again.* So I told her that my parents died in the Holocaust, 'cause I once heard somebody say that and it worked really good. She seemed pretty surprised and asked me what country that happened in. So I told her Minnesota! Boy, did she look at me strange. Up till then I was sure that a holocaust was when there was a hurricane and lots of people die, then the locusts come and eat at their dead bodies. Lucky for me I had a sneezing fit right there on the spot 'cause it kinda gave me time to think.

One time I heard this word, pickaninny. I didn't know what it meant or anything, I just liked the way it sounded. It really tickled me. So I went around calling to everybody, "Hey, your mother's a pickaninny," or "Hey, your uncle Max is a pickaninny," you know, stuff like that, till one day this big Negro boy shoved my face in. That's how I figured out its meaning. But secretly I always liked that word. So, don't ask me why, but I said to her, "Know what you are? A pickaninny!" She laughed 'cause she's smart enough to know that I was paying her a compliment.

Then she puts her hand on my shoulder real sweet-like and *again* she asks me about my mother! (*Angry.*) Well, hell's bells! That girl just don't know when to quit! What she ever do for me I'd like to know 'cept poke around into my personals. Don't even remind me, I was so mad. I jumped up and walked away, leaving her flat. I was finished with her and her lousy questions! Sinking her teeth into me. Sucking me dry. And what'd I get? A big fat nothing zero, that's what. I was doing fine before I met up with her. Just fine! Poking around my personals. Then she starts running right up next to me, which wasn't easy considering that I was walking fast and furious. But I don't pay her any mind. She asks me to stop. I don't. Then she starts pulling and pulling at my arm. That can really get on your nerves after a while. So I stop. And you know what? She's crying. Jesus Christ, she's crying. She is really crying. I can't believe it. Then she starts apologizing all over the place. Something really weird happened when I saw those tears, boy. My heart dropped straight down to my balls. Not like I wanted to do it to her or anything like that. But my thing was really sad for her. Like it wanted to cry with her. So I tell her it's okay. Then she takes my arm and it feels exactly like she and me are connected, like we're sharing the same blood. Boy, did that ever feel good.

So we walk down the hill to town and we end up at Joe's place. When Joe sees her and me arm in arm, he does one of these doubletakes. (*He does it.*) And you could tell right off the bat, he doesn't like it. So I make her sit in the photo booth whiles I go to ask Joe for a quarter. Of course he has to stick his big fat nose in and ask what this chick is doing with me. First off I tell him, "What's wrong with me?" And second off I say, "She's not a chick, she's a lady and I don't want to talk about it, so just give me the quarter and shut up." (*He giggles.*) I think he was kinda surprised 'cause I never talked to him like that before. Then he says something in a real nasty voice like, "Well, hoy de toy to you too." But he finally gives me the quarter and I slip it in the slot. Then I get in the booth with her and we get our pictures taken, smiling and making faces and all. (*He makes some grotesquely funny faces. He*

*carefully takes a photo strip from his pocket, kisses it, and places it on top
of the Temple.*)

When we got back here, know what she does? She takes my pin
from under here (*Flips his lapel.*) and pricks herself. Then she puts
her blood on the Holy Sacred Rattlesnake and Mosquito Temple.
(*Getting all choked up.*) She did that . . . (*Hysterical.*) Oh God . . . Oh
God . . . Oh God . . . (*He runs to his apple hiding place.*) Where's my
poison apple. I'm not afraid to die. (*Frantic.*) Where is it, where is
it, where *is* it? Whew! (*He retrieves the same apple the audience
member took a bite of. He shoves it into his mouth, devouring it hungrily.
Mouth full.*) If there's a God, then let this apple kill me!

(*He puts the core in his shirt pocket. He takes a pin and pricks
himself, putting the blood on the temple. Derisive.*) Ha! Ha! Ha!
Poison blood! Enjoy yourselves you little buggers! Ha Ha! That'll
teach you a thing or two, you stupid stupids!

(*He crumples to the ground in pain. He squirms and jerks in the
throes of death's agony. Suddenly he stiffens. Dead.*)

(*A few seconds of silence. He sits up. He looks around, puzzled. He
slaps himself a few times in the face.*) It didn't work . . . It didn't work.
(*Depressed.*) Aw, heck. I'm gonna live as long as a desert tortoise.
(*He takes the apple core from his pocket and digs a hole for it while
singing his Johnny Appleseed song. It sounds like he's making the words
up on the spot.*)

> Johnny Appleseed never peed
> on his own good deed.
> Oh he worked and he slaved
> and he screwed and he laid
> *And no girl ever strayed*
> from Johnny Appleseed.

(*He waters the seeds with his squirt gun. He starts doing a weird
frenzied Indian dance around the planting. He reaches a climax. He
stops suddenly. He beams.*) See! God whispers to me through my
feet. He gives me medicine. (*Bitter.*) You know what *she* thought?
She thought I drink wine all the time. I don't know what she might
have told you, but I don't. Let's just get that straight. She could be
such a big liar sometimes. Boy, could I ever use a drink now. (*He
tries to get back into his dance, but can't quite.*)

Hoi oi oi oi, Hoi oi oi oi. Her best boyfriend, huh! What does
she take me for, some kind of stupid? Who cares if a blind man
closes his eyes? That's what they all think. They send enemy

clouds. (*Shakes his fist at the sky.*) Scat! Scat! Get out of here! Or else I'm gonna make the wind blow you apart. And if you think I won't, you got another think coming!

You shoulda seen how pretty she looked coming up the path with that picnic basket. I was so happy to see her I thought I was gonna pee in my pants. *Until, until,* I see this *jerk* following behind. Guess what? Big surprise. The jerk's her boyfriend. That's what she called him. Her *boyfriend!* Can you believe it? Bringing him here, calling him that? It stinks rotten, if you ask me. I guess you couldn't exactly say I enjoyed that picnic. Matter a fact, I didn't eat a thing. Couldn't even swallow, what with the two of them getting all tangled up in each other's eyes. It made me want to throw up. I guess I made the jerk kinda uncomfortable, seeing as I wouldn't answer his jerky questions. (*Giggles.*) Every time he opened his fat trap I would make a face like this. (*He sneers.*) I couldn't help it. The guy had a talent for causing me to make faces. So pretty soon he asks her to go for a walk with him. And wouldn't you know it, they leave their garbage for me to clean up.

I wonder where they live? In pigsties, probably. So pretty soon they come back, *holding hands.* And you know what the dumb clod does? He trips over a rock. (*Proud.*) I made him do that. Then she says, "Oh, you didn't have to clean up. We would have." And the jerk says, "Yeah." Then they say their goodbyes, but I don't say nothing. She takes some leftover food from the basket and puts it down in front of me, then finally they start to leave. Know what I hear her say to her *boyfriend?* "Don't worry, honey. Sometimes he gets a little moody. He'll be all right." And where does she get off talking to some jerk about me, huh? Well maybe I won't be all right! Just maybe I won't be! Did she ever think of that? By the time they're halfway down the hill, I am so mad that I start throwing their food at them. (*Yells after them.*) What are you trying to do, poison me? I wouldn't give this to a rattlesnake . . . All of a sudden I could see their insides like I had x-ray eyes. God, was it ugly. All the shit they were carrying around inside them. Dog shit, bird shit, pig shit, fish shit floating all around in a pool of blood. (*Screams at them.*) Maggots! Maggots! Maggots! Maggots! Maggots! (*Pauses to collect himself.*)

I had to squirt water to fumigate the ground where they parked their asses. For days, weeks after that I felt like a wilted lettuce. It was all I could do to find me some grub. The rest of the time I just laid around, not hardly moving. Millions of flies and birds and crickets and spiders and mosquitos and snakes drift in and out of here, but she doesn't come. Then, all of a sudden it hits me. (*He hits his forehead as he says the words.*) You *nincom, nincom, nincom poop!* What's the matter with your brain? That's how come the jerk won her away from you! God, was I ever mad at myself. So right then and there I started looking for some smooth rocks to practice my kissing on in the hopes that some day she'd come back here. Also, I made some plans. I would go back to college and become an auto mechanic and I would give her that diamond and we would get married.

One night pretty soon after that, I start noticing that the mosquitos are making weird patterns around the Sacred Temple, and I know, don't ask my why, that she's gonna come the next day. So as soon as the sun comes up, I wait for her at the end of the path. I'm waiting and I'm waiting, and the sun is getting higher and higher and my hands are all sweaty, and my toes are all slippery and sticky, and my whole body gets soaking wet, and I don't care 'cause I know pretty soon I'm gonna see her. And I do. Coming around the bend. She gives me this wide wave like she's waving to an aeroplane. So I stick out my arms and run as fast as I can to her. (*He runs like an aeroplane, making the appropriate noise.*)

By the time I reach her I can't even talk. All I can do is grin like an idiot. So I grab her arm and start yanking her up the hill. Hey, hold your horses a minute there, she says. So I go neigh, neigh, neigh. (*He whinnies and paws the dirt.*) And she goes neigh, neigh, neigh (*He whinnies in her voice and throws back his mane.*) and we go neigh, neigh, neigh, all the way up here. And as we're standing there catching our breaths, she looks at me all soft and feathery and says, "I missed that silly face of yours." Well, that's all it took, boy. I start saying things like (*He mimics himself.*) "I missed you too, really a whole lot. All I did was think about you and make up songs about you and talk to God about you. You don't know how many ants I counted while I was missing you so much." And I go on and on and on till I have to slap my hand over my mouth to stop talking.

But she's still smiling at me. So far, so good. We're still in the ball park. Then I notice that she and me is breathing at the same time, only opposite. When I breathe out, she breathes in, and when I breathe in, she breathes out. Like we're Hansel and Gretel or Dr. Jekyll and Mr. Hyde. What I mean to say is that we belong together. So I tell her. About my plans. About me marrying her and all. Oh oh. Something's weird. All of a sudden she's not smiling any more. (*Quotations around her voice.*) "I came here because I like you and you're one of my good friends, but . . ." What kind of line is she feeding me? One of her good friends? What's going on here? Just what the heck is going on here? "I'm afraid you misunderstood me." (*Confused.*) What did she say?... What came next?... What did I do?... (*He groans, covering his face with his hands and rocking back and forth.*) Oooooh... Oooooh... Oooooh... (*Drops his hands.*)

"Please try to understand." Understand? Understand. My mind is already racing a mile a minute. (*He holds his head as if it's about to explode.*) If there is a God... If there is a God... If there is a God, then please, please, *pretty* please... (*Drops his hands.*) don't do this to me, I'm warning you. Don't you do this to me now. (*Scared.*) "Maybe I better go." Oh no you don't. You're not gonna leave your best boyfriend behind. No sir. "I'm sorry. I'm sorry. I'm *so* sorry." (*To himself.*) Okay, okay now. Gotta play your cards right. Gotta put things straight. Don't want to be counting ants this time tomorrow, do you? It's now or never, buddy boy. (*He lunges to kiss "her."*) "Aaah!... Don't... Please don't... Let me go... I didn't mean to... I never meant to... Aaaa!" (*He falls into a frenzied chant while he abuses her.*)

Damn your lies. Damn your lies. "AAAH" Damn your lies. "AAAH" Damage done. Damage done. "AAAH" Damage done. "AAAH" The goddamn damage is done and done and lies and lies and over and over and over and going up and going down and going up and going down and going up and... (*Taunting voice.*) Ain't never had a girl. *Have too.* No. You ain't never had a girl. I have too! I have too! You ain't never had a girl. (*Puts his hands over his ears.*) Lies! Filthy lies! AAAAH. (*Covers his eyes to avoid a horrible sight.*) Fire! Fire! AAAH. The crickets are popping. The spiders are melting. (*Jerks to look at the temple.*) Oh no! The temple is cracking! AAAH. (*Frantically rubs his hair.*) AAAH. Fire! Fire! She is burning my hair! Water! Quick! Come on! Hurry up! Too late! Too late! The lake is boiling! The fish are frying!

He becomes an ape beating his chest. Pauses. He becomes a stallion rearing his hooves. Panicked animals trying to escape the flames. Abruptly, he stiffens. He looks around.

He deliberately makes tracks leading from the audience to center stage. He speaks: He makes tracks. He walks back over them.

He walks back over the tracks to exit behind the audience.

THE END

Autobiography of a Pearl Diver

Martin Epstein

Autobiography of a Pearl Diver was first performed by the Magic Theatre in San Francisco. The production opened April 27, 1979, with the following cast:

JOYCE	Linda Hoy
P.H.	Abe Kalish
BINGO KARP	Rick Prindle
BILL	Peter Coyote

Directed by Andrew Doe
Designed by Michael Kroschel
Lighting by Ron Madonia
Costumes by Suresa Dundes
Sound by Robert Welles

CHARACTERS

P.H.: Retired attorney, early sixties. Slow, shrewd, self-satisfied.
JOYCE: His wife, late fifties. She holds her breath.
BINGO KARP: An alcoholic cop and friend of the family, late fifties.
BILL: AAA mechanic, early thirties.

SCENE

A residential neighborhood.

TIME

The recent past.

Photos courtesy of Magic Theatre.

Autobiography of a Pearl Diver

Martin Epstein

Complete darkness.

The lights of an aquarium blink on. A medium-sized aquarium, the fish visible, a very faint hum.

Stage lights up, slow, a living room adjacent to kitchen. Several hanging plants. A sofa, chairs, a cabinet with china, a few books, a TV *set, etc. Door to bathroom, rear or side.*

Upstage wall of house entirely of glass. A sliding glass door looks out on patio. Flowers, grass, a fence, a tree with a thick trunk.

An early Sunday morning in April. Birds. P.H. *visible in bathroom, brushing his teeth, gargling.*

JOYCE: (*Off.*) Peeeeee Aaaaaaitch?

P.H. *shakes brush dry, emerges, looks about, goes to fish tank, feeds fish, making little nibbling sounds.*

JOYCE: (*Off.*) Peeeee Aaaaaaitch?

Newspaper thrown over fence, hits glass wall. P.II. *goes to door, retrieves it.*

JOYCE: (*Off.*) Peeeee Aaaitch!

P.H.: (*Coming back into room, looking through paper.*) Good old Joyce. I generally answer her every third or fourth call. Otherwise she'd have me jumping round this place like a trained dog.

JOYCE: (*Off.*) Peeeee ... (*Her voice cracks.*)

P.H. *takes his seat, glances through paper.* JOYCE *appears outside glass. She is holding a birthday cake. The candles have been burned, down to the quick. She enters the house.*

P.H.: Morning, dear.

JOYCE: (*Sets cake on table, lightly.*) Didn't you hear me calling you?

P.H.: Yes.

JOYCE: Why didn't you answer?

P.H.: I was working up to it.

JOYCE: (*Moves to kitchen, searches, finds a large candle.*) And I was working up to shouting myself hoarse.

P.H.: Well, it's the Sabbath, Joyce.

JOYCE: What's the Sabbath got to do with anything?

P.H.: God's day of rest. Those of us made in his image are commanded to do the same.

JOYCE: God only rested one day a week. How come you take off all seven?

P.H.: Maybe I'm smarter. (*Turns page.*) Oh, thanks for the birthday cake. It's a beauty.

JOYCE: I had a present for you out in the garage.

P.H.: Did you?

JOYCE: You can kiss it goodbye, though.

P.H.: How come?

JOYCE: Those who don't respond when they're called don't get presents. (*She grinds the candle at a slightly rakish angle into the cake.*)

P.H.: Hm. Well, I guess that's that. No present.

JOYCE: Aren't you at all curious to know what you missed?

P.H.: No. Last night a fellow turned up the wrong ramp of the freeway and drove sixteen miles against the oncoming traffic.

JOYCE: It was really going to be some gift!

P.H.: I'm sure. (*Sips coffee.*) Seven dead. Eleven injured. Five critically. He got off without a scratch. A history professor.

JOYCE: It was going to be the surprise of your life, P.H.

P.H.: Yes? Well, after my little peck of heart trouble last winter, maybe it's best I shy away from anything that might overstimulate my imagination.

JOYCE: I was going to gas myself. (*Pause.*) I said I was going to gas myself.

P.H.: And that was going to be your present?

JOYCE: No. That was going to be *your* present.

P.H.: I'm not sure I understand you, Joyce.

JOYCE: Last night, after I took the trash out, I went into the garage, turned on the ignition, and sat there a good ten minutes, breathing fumes. *You understand that?*

P.H.: Yes. (*Pause.*) What went wrong?

JOYCE: I couldn't find anything I wanted to listen to on the radio. I wanted some music. Something quiet and sad. Some classical piece. But there was only a hockey game. And a Bible preacher.

And a news broadcast. And some fools going on about reincarnation and hot tubs and the Chinese *Book of Changes*. And it was too dark. And too cold. And I got to thinking I'd much rather gas myself with the sun coming up. So I decided to postpone it till just now.

P.H.: What went wrong?

JOYCE: I couldn't start the car.

P.H.: How come?

JOYCE: The battery's dead.

P.H.: The battery?

JOYCE: (*Embarrassed.*) I left the lights on.

P.H.: All night?

JOYCE: Well, I was dizzy.

P.H.: Did you remember to turn them off just now?

JOYCE: (*Pause.*) I don't remember.

P.H.: You still dizzy, Joyce?

JOYCE: No. Depressed. (*Holds breath. Lets breath go.*) I'm very depressed.

P.H.: Yes, well, let's just get out the old AAA card and give the folks at the garage a little call. (*He gets out card, extends it to her.*)

JOYCE: You phone them. I'm not having anything to do with it. (*He dials phone.*) Doesn't anything ever get under your skin?

P.H.: Remember when you married me, Joyce, I asked you what it was you most admired about my character. You said, my "tolerance." (*On phone.*) Hello . . . yes . . . would you send a repair truck to 41 Denton Drive. My wife left the lights on all night and now the battery's dead. . . . 54533124F. . . . Thanks. (*Hangs up.*) Terrific people, the AAA. Probably the only organization left in this country a man can still depend on.

JOYCE: Did you have to tell them I left the lights on?

P.H.: Well, you did, didn't you?

JOYCE: Yes. But did you have to go out of your way to embarrass me?

P.H.: I wasn't going out of my way, Joyce.

JOYCE: Suppose I left them on on purpose?

P.H.: To kill the battery, Joyce?

JOYCE: To save my life, P.H.!

P.H.: Well, I guess you succeeded.

JOYCE: Yes, I guess I did.

P.H.: It's definite, then?

JOYCE: What?

P.H.: You're not going to give it another try?

JOYCE: No, I don't think I will.

P.H.: How come?

JOYCE: Well, P.H., I just now realized my death would have been completely wasted on you.

P.H.: What makes you say that?

JOYCE: Because you wouldn't have really missed me.

P.H.: (*Pause.*) What makes you say that?

JOYCE: You never missed B.F.

P.H.: (*Pause.*) B.F. doesn't deserve to be missed.

JOYCE: Seven whole years away from home and not one day goes by in which you've ever really missed him.

P.H.: That's not a fair statement, Joyce. I think about B.F. all the time.

JOYCE: But you don't actually miss him!

P.H.: Well, he doesn't miss me, either, Joyce.

JOYCE: For a very good reason.

P.H.: And sometimes I wonder if he even misses you.

JOYCE: Oh, he misses me, all right. He said so when he wrote.

P.H.: One damn postcard in seven years isn't what I'd call a testament to his filial devotion, Joyce.

JOYCE: It was a beautiful postcard.

P.H.: Not even a return address.

JOYCE: When you're on a yacht in the middle of the Indian Ocean...

P.H.: (*Anger.*) Let's drop the subject, shall we?

JOYCE: (*Pause.*) And he went through the trouble to have his picture taken and made into the postcard.

P.H.: That wasn't his picture.

JOYCE: It most definitely was his picture.

P.H.: (*Pause.*) The fellow in that picture had a body.

JOYCE: A mother knows her own son, P.H. Even in dark glasses and a suntan.

P.H.: My mother didn't know me at the end. Looked up at me from her bed like I was a complete stranger.

JOYCE: Maybe that's what you were...

P.H.: Maybe that's what he is.

JOYCE: As for his filling out, it's natural. All that sea and sky and sun. All that exercise. (*Pause.*) You're just jealous.

P.H.: Of what?

JOYCE: The fact he had his arm around that lovely dark girl.

P.H.: Black, Joyce. That lovely black girl.

JOYCE: Well, that's the normal skin color in that part of the world.

P.H.: And the normal occupation, too, I suppose?

JOYCE: Pearl diving, yes.

P.H.: (*Snorts.*) Pearl diving!

JOYCE: Just because you wanted him to study law...

P.H.: Look, I never gave a damn what he studied!

JOYCE: Diving for pearls is a much more exotic profession.

P.H.: Diving for pearls isn't a profession, Joyce. It's an idiocy.

JOYCE: All he'd have to do is come up with one good-sized pearl, and you wouldn't call it such an idiocy.

P.H.: One good-sized pearl! (*Laughs.*) What size pearl is that? A pearl the size of my head, I suppose!

JOYCE: No. They don't come that big.

P.H.: A pearl the size of your head, then!

JOYCE: More like the size of an egg.

P.H.: An egg?

JOYCE: Yes. A pearl the size of an egg. You know, the kind chickens lay?

P.H.: (*Pause.*) You can't let that old egg rest, can you, Joyce?

JOYCE: I can't imagine to what you're referring.

P.H.: I am referring, as well you know, to the PAL Olympics at Mt. Carmel Stadium, Joyce. I am referring to the egg B.F. and I passed back and forth that bright, sunny day so many years ago in the father-son egg-throw contest.

JOYCE: (*Singsong.*) I wasn't thinking of that egg at all.

P.H.: (*Singsong.*) Oh yes you were.

JOYCE: (*Singsong.*) You must have a guilty conscience.

P.H.: (*Singsong.*) There's nothing for me to feel guilty about.

JOYCE: (*Singsong.*) Are you sure?

P.H.: I told B.F. before the contest began. I took him around the shoulder and I told him: "B.F., all you have to do is concentrate. Think. Don't let anyone faze you. No one rush you. The whole secret of success is concentrated effort coupled with an unfailing desire to win." And then the whistle blew and the forty of us father-son teams lined up adjacent to each other, and the ref fired the gun. BANG! (*He makes tossing gesture, accompanied by a sound.*) Each time we completed a pass (*He receives egg, catching it gracefully.*) we both took one step back. (*He passes off egg.*) I can't tell you how my heart was pounding, Joyce. All around us eggs flying by. Eggs shattering on the ground, in the hand. Jesus! And

the crowd cheering. And the distance between me and B.F.
growing so huge it felt like there was a whole continent between
us. And then just the two of us out there on the long green with
one other couple. And the whole stadium counting—"Seventeen!" "Yea!" "Eighteen!" "Yea!" "Nineteen!" "Yea!" (*He re-
ceives, tosses off with each count.*) And then it was just B.F. and me
and one lone egg (*He tosses it off.*) sailing through the sky in a
great smooth arc. And all he had to do was catch the damn thing
one more time!
JOYCE: But he didn't catch it!
P.H.: No, he didn't.
JOYCE: He dropped it!
P.H.: Yes, he did!
JOYCE: And more than seven hundred people saw it bounce!
P.H.: (*Innocent.*) I had no idea at all it was a rubber egg, Joyce.
JOYCE: You did.
P.H.: It was B.F.'s idea entirely.
JOYCE: Liar. There was money involved.
P.H.: B.F. confessed. He bought it in the five-and-dime.
JOYCE: Only to save your reputation! You were running for district
    attorney at the time!
P.H.: Look. The whole incident was entirely inconsequential.
    Everyone laughed. A rubber egg. They all thought it was funny.
JOYCE: An eleven-year-old boy is humiliated in front of seven
    hundred people, and everyone thinks it's funny!
P.H.: Anyway, I lost that damn election!
JOYCE: And B.F. lost his faith in life!
P.H.: Oh, hell!

Doorbell.

JOYCE: Quit his Little League team!
P.H.: Go answer the door.
JOYCE: Couldn't keep his mind on his school studies!

Doorbell.

P.H.: Joyce . . .
JOYCE: Dropped Stuart Boysie, his best friend, and was ashamed to
    have anyone over to the house!
P.H.: It's probably the mechanic!

Doorbell.

JOYCE: Crept in and out for the next seven years like a thief!

Doorbell.

P.H.: Will you answer the door, for chrissake!

JOYCE: And when he couldn't stand it anymore, he left!

Enter KARP, *from side. Full police uniform.*

KARP: I take the liberty of entering unannounced. You shouldn't keep the side door open. There are lots of maniacs running around. Morning, Joyce. (*No response.*) Morning, Pat?

P.H.: Morning, Bingo! What gets you up so early?

KARP: You read the paper yet?

P.H.: Some.

KARP: The professor . . .

P.H.: The one who drove twelve miles against the traffic?

KARP: They're holding him down at the station. He wasn't drunk, and he won't say a word. So before we tear up his driver's license, the boys would like me to see what I can do.

P.H.: Think you'll get him to open up?

KARP: Twenty bucks says I will.

JOYCE: You going to beat him up, Bingo?

P.H.: Oh Joyce.

KARP: Someday I hope someone comes along who can really explain the whole business of being a cop to a very misinformed public.

JOYCE: You put them in your circle, don't you? You put them in your circle, and then you take turns.

P.H.: Joyce . .

KARP: If you were in the circle, Joyce, you'd see it from a whole different point of view.

JOYCE: What point of view is that?

KARP: I'll tell you. We had this Mexican kid in one time. He broke up a bar over some girl! He wrote poetry. Anyway, he asked to go to the bathroom. We let him, and he climbed out the window and shimmied up a drain pipe. For a few minutes we thought we'd lost him. Which is very bad, because everyone gets docked a week's pay if anyone escapes. So when we caught him, finally, on the roof, we brought him down and put him in the circle. I wish you could have been there, Joyce.

JOYCE: Why?

KARP: After we'd gone round twice, he's smiling. Later on, I gave
him a cigarette. Asked him what he was smiling about. He said
after the first round, he began feeling like we were all his broth-
thers. It was like a rite, he said. And he loved us.

P.H.: He must have been a poet.

KARP: I liked him a lot, too. (*Takes package from coat.*) Oh, say, this
is for you, Pat. With many happy returns of the day.

P.H.: Thanks, Bingo. (*Having undone package.*) Let's see what you've
brought me here. Look, Joyce. A whole fifth of Bushmill's Irish
Whiskey.

KARP: Paradise in a shot glass, Pat.

JOYCE: He can't drink it.

P.H.: Oh hell.

JOYCE: The doctor said . . .

KARP: I clean forgot about your heart, Pat.

P.H.: A thimbleful now and then!

KARP: (*Reaching for bottle.*) No, no, no, it's absolutely out of the
question! A man doesn't have that many good friends he can
afford to push the very best of them into the hereafter. (*Pulling
on bottle.*) Give up that bottle, damn you. (*Pulls it free.*)

P.H.: You going to exchange it, Bingo?

KARP: Exchange a fifth of Bushmill's? For what? Joyce, you got a
nice clean shot glass?

JOYCE: All my glasses are clean, Bingo. (*She goes to kitchen.*)

KARP: She's a bit nippy this morning, eh?

P.H.: Am I going to get another present?

KARP: Next year for sure.

P.H.: That's the second present I lost this morning.

KARP: Yeah, well. Off the record, Pat, if you were to tell me that
heart condition of yours was just your little way of retiring ten
years earlier on a full salary from the city, I'd be more than glad
to share this bottle with ya.

P.H.: Off the record, Bingo, suppose I were really faking it, what
would you do?

KARP: Off the record, Pat, I'd turn you in first chance I got. (*Both
men laugh.* JOYCE *returns with two shot glasses.*)

JOYCE: I'd like one, too.

P.H.: Since when do you drink?

JOYCE: I'd like one, too.

P.H.: Pour her a drink. (BINGO *pours.*)

KARP: Sure would be nice to pour one of these out for your old

man, too, Joyce. Too bad he's sick. Cheers, Pat. (*He drinks.* JOYCE
holds her drink before her.)

P.H.: Well, you going to drink it or stare at it like it was your urine
specimen? (JOYCE *sets the full glass down.*)

KARP: Change your mind, Joyce? (*Silence. He picks up glass.*) I don't
like to see the stuff evaporate. (*Drinks, sighs.*) God, it buzzes
through you, just like magic.

P.H.: I've never met anyone who could put it away like you, Bingo.
· And it never seems to faze you.

KARP: (*Pouring out two more glasses.*) I'll tell you something that
does faze me, Pat. The latest statistics on the rising crime rate.
Right there next to our professor's photograph. (*He picks up one
glass, drinks, sets it down.*) Everything's up. Muggings. Robberies.
Rape. Fraud. Murder. (*Lifts second glass.*) I did a little quick figur-
ing on my pocket calculator. Do you realize, if the statistics con-
tinue to climb at *half* the present rate, by the year two thousand,
every man, woman and child in America will be engaged in some
kind of criminal activity?

JOYCE: Even the police?

KARP: (*Looks at her. Drinks.*)

P.H.: I'm kind of glad I won't be around to see it.

KARP: You know, Pat, sometimes I believe your interest in the law
was never based on anything except your own personal ambition.

P.H.: I'd be the very last one to deny it, Bingo.

KARP: (*Pours two more glasses.*) Don't you give a good goddamn
about the future, Pat?

P.H.: Frankly, no.

KARP: Well, I do. (*Drinks.*) I goddamnit do. (*Drinks.*) Me and
Douglas MacArthur. We care about tomorrow.

P.H.: Is that the "Back to Bataan" MacArthur you're talking about?

KARP: Nineteen fifty-three, when Ike took office. Just after the
Korean debacle. MacArthur came to him, a civilian. Took him by
the shoulders. Looked him in the eye. (*Pours a bit on table, stops,
moves glass over, pours into glass.*) Says, "Ike! Ike, goddamnit!
Ike! (*Pause.*) Ike, the salvation of America and the entire free
world is in your hands." (*Pause.*) "Ike, you've got to nip them in
the bud!"

JOYCE: Nip who in the bud?

KARP: The Chinese Communists, Joyce.

JOYCE: Oh.

KARP: "Three well-placed cobalt bombs along the Yalu, Ike!"

JOYCE: What's a cobalt bomb?

KARP: "Three cobalt bombs along the Yalu will send them all back to the cave man era. And after that, we won't have to worry about the sons of bitches for another ten to twenty thousand years!"

JOYCE: What's a cobalt bomb?

KARP: But do you think anyone took old Mac's advice? War Monger they called him. Lunatic, Bastard, Sadist they called him. Old Soldier, they called him. And twenty years later Nixon has to sit down at the same table and *eat* with them! He's got to *eat* with a people whose ideology we basically despise. (*Sighs, stares at glass.*) Now I ask you, is anything to be learned from this experience?

P.H.: Bingo, are you advocating we drop a cobalt bomb on the entire criminal population of the United States?

KARP: Don't be an ass, Pat. (*Leaning in.*) But that is not to say we should not be making plans to secure the entire country in one enormous penintential compound!

P.H.: The innocent along with the guilty?

KARP: *There are no more innocent, Pat! Look!* (*More reasonable.*) If a horse drinks from the same trough as a pig, could we not say that horse has become a bit of a pig?

P.H.: Why not say the pig's become a bit of a horse?

KARP: Don't confuse the issue with your courtroom shenanigans, Pat. The single most difficult task in this country today, besides an all-out war on crime, is to stick to the goddamn point!

JOYCE: What's a cobalt bomb?

P.H.: You know the problem with you, Karp?

KARP: Problem?

P.H.: You should have gotten married.

KARP: (*Stares at him.*) What the hell has marriage got to do with anything?

P.H.: A man without a wife and kids can well afford to care about the future. (*He pours himself a shot, drinks.*)

KARP: That's not a very nice thing to say about marriage, Pat. Particularly in the presence of your lovely spouse. What's your response to a statement like that, Joyce?

JOYCE: Is suicide considered a criminal activity?

KARP: Only when it's unsuccessful. Why?

JOYCE: I tried to gas myself last night.

P.H.: This morning, too.

JOYCE: Yes. This morning, too. I tried twice.

KARP: You're pulling my leg, Joyce.

JOYCE: Ask him.

P.H.: It's true, Bingo. She tried twice.

JOYCE: Am I under arrest, Bingo?

KARP: (*Looks at* P.H.) What's goin' on?

P.H.: She wants to know if she's under arrest.

KARP: Tell her, I can't arrest her.

JOYCE: Why not?

KARP: Because you're my friend, Joyce.

JOYCE: I am not your friend, Bingo! P.H. is your friend! I'm just his wife. I'm the wife who tried to gas herself.

P.H.: Twice.

KARP: What the hell is going on here?

P.H.: Arrest her, Bingo. Take her downtown and throw her in the tank with the whores!

KARP: Are you guys serious?

JOYCE: I am!

P.H.: Me too!

KARP: But we don't throw attempted suicides in the tank with the whores.

JOYCE: What do you do with them?

KARP: We put them under psychiatric observation.

JOYCE: Yes. That's just what I want. I want to be put under psychiatric observation.

KARP: I must be dreaming. (*Pours another glass.*)

P.H.: (*Indicating glass.*) Me, too.

KARP: (*Pours into* P.H.'*s glass.*) Why'd she try to gas herself, Pat?

JOYCE: Why do you ask him? I'm right here!

KARP: Why'd she try to gas herself, Pat?

P.II.: It was going to be my birthday present.

KARP: Why'd you try to gas yourself, Joyce?

JOYCE: It was going to be his birthday present. (KARP *raises drink to mouth, lowers it.*) I'd have carried it through, too. Only I realized he wouldn't have missed me.

P.H.: I'd have missed her, all right.

JOYCE: He's never paid any real attention to me.

P.H.: You gonna drink that? (*Pause.* KARP *looks at him.* P.H. *takes* KARP'*s glass, swallows it down.*)

JOYCE: When P.H. was courting me, I made it my business to read every book I could find on the Mafia. Because I knew he was interested in criminal law, and I wanted him to know I was interested in what he was interested in.

P.H.: I think it's time we ate that cake! Where's the cake knife? (*Riffling through drawer.*)

JOYCE: I must have read twenty-five or thirty books on the Mafia.

P.H.: (*With knife.*) You want a piece of birthday cake, Bingo? (*Pause.* BINGO *stares.*) Bingo?

KARP: Sure.

JOYCE: Ask him how many books he read about the things I was interested in!

P.H.: (*Slicing cake.*) They don't write books about nothing, Joyce. Unless you're talking about that one that broke all the best-seller records—what was it called now?

KARP: *Gone with the Wind.*

P.H.: No. *The Autobiography of a Pearl Diver.*

KARP: Never heard of it.

P.H.: Because you're an illiterate.

KARP: I'm not an illiterate. I just don't read. What's it about, Pat?

P.H.: It's about this kid whose mother poisons his heart against his father.

KARP: Mothers like that should be sent to the chair.

P.H.: His father's life's not good enough.

KARP: His father's house not good enough. Any wonder the kid slinks around like a thief.

P.H.: Any wonder he's never there when you need him.

KARP: Any wonder he's like a kamikaze in slow motion, out to blow himself and his whole life to smithereens!

JOYCE: B.F. is not a kamikaze.

P.H.: Don't talk, Joyce, you haven't read the book.

JOYCE: Wherever he is, he's leading a richer life than either of you are even capable of imagining.

P.H.: Ohhhh . . .

KARP: Ouuuu . . .

JOYCE: A good life, a full life . . .

P.H.: Sure, sure. Long ecstatic days chasing after dolphins.

KARP: Exotic nights of love in Moroccan alleyways.

P.H.: A pearl through his ear and a pearl through his nose . . .

KARP: Pockets full of pearls . . .

P.H.: Turbaned in silk like some prince from the Arabian Nights . . .

KARP: Wherever he goes, the sound of pearls bouncing on sidewalks . . .

P.H.: Hordes of destitute children follow him around, scooping them up in their bony little fists.

KARP: Princess Grace has him over for dinner.

P.H.: Picasso takes him to a bullfight.

KARP: Mailer does an article on his sex life.

P.H.: Pacino begs them in Hollywood to play the role.

KARP: There's a huge parade down Fifth Avenue. All New York turns out. Tell them, Pat. Tell about the huge parade down Fifth Avenue. Like the one they had for Kennedy . . . (*Pause.* P.H. *rubbing his heart.*) What's the matter, Pat?

P.H.: Nothing. (*Moody, saddened.*) You tell it.

KARP: Standing like a young god in the open motorcade, he lifts both hands in the air, and guess what falls from the sky? (*Pause.*) Pearls. Pearls pour down from the sky.

P.H.: Pearls . . .

KARP: Pearls by the billions pour down from the sky. New York is covered under a white blanket of pearls. B.F. gets Jackie O. for the night. He gives it to her up the old wazoo! (*Laughs. Silence.*) Tell what happens next, Pat.

P.H.: What happens next? The prodigal comes home. Having gratified himself and his desires, he decides to pay a visit to his quite ordinary inconsequential folks in the suburbs. Drives up in his silver Mercedes, parks a whole block away, so the neighbors won't recognize him. Walks the distance, trying to gather the courage to face his old father. His old sick father, gasping away the last of his lonely days in bed.

KARP: Unnnn.

P.H.: Poisoned by his mother's bad mouth and stricken with grief that his only begotten son has exiled himself in a world of pure fantasy. (*To* JOYCE.) For none of it is real, except the knock on the door. (KARP *knocks on the table.*) "Come in, son. I've been waiting a long time for this moment!" the father speaking.

KARP: The father speaking.

P.H.: "Throw a handful of pearls to your mother, there, 'cause that's what she expects. But as for me, I want you to answer one simple question."

KARP: "What question is that, Pop?"

P.H.: "Are you a man, son?"

KARP: (*Pause.*) "What's a man, Pop?"

P.H.: "A man is someone who knows how to slug it out in the real world."

KARP: "You want a few pearls, Pop?"

P.H.: (*Hitting his hand.*) "Don't gimme that shit! I'm telling you a man is someone who learns at an early age that people, given the chance, will lie, cheat, steal, and even kill everything you hold near and dear unless you're right there to defend it with your life!"

KARP: (*To* JOYCE.) If only he'd been this eloquent in the courtroom.

P.H.: (*To* KARP, *directly.*) *A man does not hide out in some obscure corner of his life and pretend he couldn't care less what others think of him!*

JOYCE: A man like you!

P.H.: A man like me, that's right! (*Silence.* P.H. *rubs his heart.*)

KARP: Nice cake. (P.H. *pours another glass.*) You'd better go easy.

P.H.: Shut up. (*Drinks.* JOYCE *goes over to fish tank, picks up food.*) I already fed them. (*She taps in food.*) You'll kill them you feed them any more. They'll swell up on you and burst! (*She puts food down.*) (*To* KARP.) She never feeds them when they need feeding. When they need feeding, I'm the one who feeds them.

JOYCE: I'm the one who loves them!

P.H.: She loves them, but she starves them!

JOYCE: I get angry sometimes. (*Silence.*)

KARP: Shall we drink to tropical fish, mates?

P.H.: To the topical tropicals, right! (*They clink glasses.*)

KARP: I wonder what it must be like to do nothing but eat, shit and swim around all day enclosed by four glass walls?

P.H.: Ask my wife.

JOYCE: What do you know about them? Or about me, for that matter?

P.H.: I know what I see!

JOYCE: What you see isn't all there is!

P.H.: What I see is all I care about!

JOYCE: You don't care about very much!

P.H.: I care about what interests me, Joyce.

JOYCE: Well, let me tell you, these fish are every bit as interesting as the Mafia.

P.H.: But not nearly as dangerous, eh, Karp?

KARP: There's always the piranha.

P.H.: Joyce doesn't have any piranha in her tank. She keeps community fish only.

JOYCE: What are they?

P.H.: Fish that can live peacefully together in the same tank.

KARP: Sounds like pretty dull stuff. (*Looking at fish.*) What this tank needs is a piranha or two to liven these community fish up a bit. Look at the bastards. (*Tapping tank with his shot glass.*) They're too lethargic to react. (*Taps.*) Jump, you bastards! (*Taps.*) Jump! Come on! Jump! Oops, there they go! (*Taps.*) Fear, ha! (*Taps.*) Fear!

JOYCE: Leave them alone, Bingo!

MECHANIC *appears outside, taps on door.* BINGO, *startled, whirls, drawing out his gun.*

JOYCE & P.II.: Bingo!

MECHANIC *raises his hands above his head.*

MECHANIC: Did someone send for a mechanic?

KARP: (*To* P.H.) You expecting a mechanic?

P.H.: Yes.

JOYCE: Put that gun away, you fool.

KARP: Don't call me a fool, Joyce. I was trying to protect what's yours. (*Holsters gun.*)

P.H.: (*Opening door.*) Come on in. You can put your hands down. He's not dangerous.

KARP: Sure. I'm a real pussycat.

MECHANIC: A dead battery, they said.

P.H.: (*Pointing to* JOYCE.) Hers.

MECHANIC: Yours?

JOYCE: (*To herself.*) I want to go downtown. I want to be put under 'psychiatric observation.

KARP: Yeah, sure, Joyce. Me, too.

P.H.: Joyce, why don't you go shopping or something? (JOYCE *looks at him, coldly. Silence.*)

MECHANIC: A dead battery, they said.

P.H.: (*Pause.*) Bingo, offer the young man a drink.

KARP: I don't know if I want to share my bottle with this guy.

P.H.: He's all right.

KARP: You sure?

P.H.: He's come to charge my battery.

KARP: Oh. Okay. We'll give him a thimbleful.

MECHANIC: (*Still outside.*) Thanks, no. It's kinda early.

KARP: Early for you, maybe. (*He drinks.*)

JOYCE: My hands are trembling.

P.H.: What about a cup of coffee, then? And a piece of cake.

MECHANIC: (*Leaning in.*) A cup of coffee and a piece of cake. (*Pause.*) What kind of cake?

P.H.: Chocolate.

MECHANIC: (*Deliberating.*) Chocolate. (*Steps inside.*) Okay.

P.H.: Joyce, why don't you fit the young man out with some cake and coffee?

JOYCE: (*Looking at her hands.*) No.

P.H.: No?

JOYCE: Let the young man fit himself out with some cake and coffee.

MECHANIC: It's okay, Ma'am. I'm an old pro with a cake knife. (*Picks up knife, measures piece. Cuts.*)

P.H.: That's a pretty big piece you cut there.

MECHANIC: Too big?

P.H.: Why don't you just take half of that. (MECHANIC *measures out half, cuts.*)

KARP: Why don't you just take half of that? (MECHANIC *smiles, cuts second piece in half. It's rather small.* KARP *eats the other slices.*)

MECHANIC: (*Watches* BINGO *eat his cake.*) Won't you get sick if you mix it with whiskey?

KARP: Mix what?

MECHANIC: Chocolate cake and whiskey.

KARP: (*Eating.*) You a mechanic or a dietitian?

MECHANIC: (*Eats his cake.*) Mechanic. What do you do for a living?

P.H.: Coffee's on the stove.

MECHANIC: (*Getting coffee.*) Someone's birthday today?

P.H.: Mine.

MECHANIC: Happy birthday.

P.H.: Thanks.

MECHANIC: How old?

P.H.: None of your business.

JOYCE: He's sixty-two.

MECHANIC: Jesus. You look a lot younger.

P.H.: Thanks.

MECHANIC: People say I don't look my age, either.

JOYCE: How old?

MECHANIC: Thirty-six.

JOYCE: They're right. You've got the face of a boy, still.

MECHANIC: Yeah.

KARP: What's your beauty secret?

MECHANIC: I try to keep my stress level down. The way I see it, if you let yourself in for tension, you gotta age.

KARP: You gotta age anyway.

MECHANIC: True. But there's aging, and there's aging.

KARP: I'm a cop. My life is constant tension.

JOYCE: I wouldn't take you for more than twenty-five.

KARP: Who, me?

JOYCE: Him. Twenty-five. B.F.'s age.

MECHANIC: B.F.?

JOYCE: My son.

KARP: Butter Fingers.

JOYCE: His name isn't Butter Fingers, Bingo.

KARP: B.F. Butter Fingers.

JOYCE: I'll thank you to stop calling him that!

KARP: I didn't invent it, Joyce. He earned it. After the egg-throw fiasco. We lost a bundle on that one, didn't we, Pat? Two hundred bucks apiece, plus a buck forty-nine for the rubber egg!

P.H.: I lost the district attorneyship! (*To* MECHANIC.) B.F. was named for a great American patriot.

KARP: Make him guess, Pat. Let's see if he's up on his history.

P.H.: (*Pause.*) He wrote the Declaration of Independence.

MECHANIC: B.F.?

KARP: Invented the bifocal? (*Pause.*) Flew his kite in a storm with a key attached to the tail? (*Pause.*)

MECHANIC: I been out of school a long time.

KARP: It's a good thing you were born in this country.

JOYCE: Benjamin Franklin.

MECHANIC: Benjamin Franklin. Hm. Sure. (*Pause.*) And here, all along, I thought it was Thomas Jefferson wrote the Declaration of Independence.

P.H. AND KARP: What?

MECHANIC: Nothin'.

JOYCE: Benjamin Franklin Bibbs.

MECHANIC: Bibbs?

JOYCE: My husband's name is Bibbs. (*Laughs.*) My maiden name was Salem. Which do you like better?

MECHANIC: Salem.

P.H.: Nevertheless, the law says Bibbs. (*Laughs, imitating her laugh.*)

KARP: Benjamin Franklin Butter Fingers Bibbs.

JOYCE: P.H.'s father was a high school civics teacher. All of his eight brothers and sisters were named for American patriots. P.H. thought if he named his own son patriotically, his father would leave him some money.

P.H.: Joyce . . .

JOYCE: Things did not work out that way, however. I was dead set against Benjamin Franklin. I wanted to name him Terrence. But money won out in the end. Though the old man didn't leave a dime to any of them. (*Laughs.*) And P.H. ended up having to pay the entire cost of his funeral.

P.H.: Joyce . . .

MECHANIC: What's the P.H. stand for?

KARP: "Give me liberty or give me death."

P.H.: That's enough out of you, Karp!

MECHANIC: "Give me liberty or give me death"?

JOYCE: Spoken on the floor of the first Constitutional Congress in 1776. Right, P.H.?

KARP: (*Laughs; drinks.*) Christ, I'm pissed!

JOYCE: Patrick Henry spoke those words.

MECHANIC: (*Pause.*) So which did he get, liberty or death?

JOYCE: Ask P.H. He's the intellectual in this family.

MECHANIC: Which did he get, Mr. Bibbs?

P.H.: He got both.

MECHANIC: Both?

P.H.: He got his liberty, and then he died.

MECHANIC: Yeah, well . . . (*Eats cake.*) Life's a bitch sometimes. (*Puts down cup, starts for door.*) Well, that battery . . .

P.H.: First he eats, and then he runs.

KARP: What's your name, greaseball?

MECHANIC: Bill.

KARP: Bill!

BILL: In certain circles I'm known as W.B.

JOYCE: W.B.?

BILL: Want a clue?

JOYCE: Yes.

BILL: Famous American cowboy, cleared the west of buffalo and Indians.

KARP: Buffalo Bill!

JOYCE: That's B.B., Bingo. He said his initials are W.B.

BILL: You all give up? (*Silence.*) Wild Bill.

KARP: Wild Bill.

BILL: (*Smiling.*) An early girlfriend named me that.

KARP: How early?

BILL: She was fourteen.

KARP: Fourteen. They have laws on the books about that kind of thing.

BILL: I don't think she'd issue a complaint, Sheriff.

P.H.: And the name stuck all this time?

BILL: Yep. Say, you mind if I cut myself another slice of cake? That last one was awfully small.

P.H.: No more cake!

JOYCE: Would you like a fork, Wild Bill?

BILL: No, Ma'am. My fingers will do, if no one objects. (*He cuts, then takes an enormous slice. Eats.*)

JOYCE: Is that a wedding ring, Wild Bill?

BILL: (*Eating.*) Um hm.

KARP: So a woman managed to corral you after all, eh, Wild Bill?

BILL: Yeah. Close to seven years' worth.

P.H.: Does she also call you Wild Bill?

BILL: No, sir. She calls me Mr. Filth.

JOYCE: Mr. Filth?

BILL: On account of my hands and the grease from the cars. Which is, ya know, difficult sometimes to get off, particularly if I'm hungry or going to bed and don't want to spend an hour scrubbing up in the bathroom in order to satisfy my basic appetites.

KARP: His basic appetites.

JOYCE: Any children, Wild Bill?

BILL: No children, Ma'am. And as of last week, no wife, either.

JOYCE: No wife?

BILL: She split.

JOYCE: Oh, I'm sorry.

BILL: Yeah, well . . .

JOYCE: Is it a permanent separation?

BILL: (*Pause.*) Permanent?

JOYCE: I mean is she coming back?

BILL: Probably not. She took everything except the fish.

JOYCE: You have fish?

BILL: She does.

JOYCE: Tropical fish?

BILL: Yeah.

JOYCE: I have fish, too.

KARP: Dull community fish. (*Belches.*)

BILL: So I noticed. (*Moves toward tank.*) Your tank, if you don't

mind my saying so, could use a cleaning. I mean, you see the way
that molly is swimming a forty-degree angle. She's not going to
live through the night.

JOYCE: A lot of them are dying off.

P.H.: She loves them, but I'm the one who feeds them.

BILL: (*To* JOYCE.) What you should do is get yourself a plecostomus.

JOYCE: A plecostomus?

BILL: They've got mouths like a toilet sponge. They'll eat all this
algae, suck it right off the glass. Oh, say, look here. This one's
finished. (*He dips net, scoops out dead fish.*)

JOYCE: It's my blind cave fish.

BILL: (*Takes fish by tail.*) Poor bastard. Ya know, whenever I take a
close look at one of these things, I get a really weird sensation.
It's like I see the whole race of them, all at once. Them and their
mothers and fathers, and their mothers' and fathers' mothers and
fathers, going all the way back to the beginning of time. Ten or
twenty million years have passed and nothing's changed.

P.H.: They've made no progress, huh?

BILL: None whatsoever.

KARP: That's why they deserve to be eaten on Fridays.

BILL: What do you want me to do with him?

JOYCE: I generally flush them down the toilet.

P.H.: An ignominious end.

BILL: Shall we give this one to the birds? (*Slides open door, tosses it
out.*) Keep the food chain going, fella. (*Slides door closed.*)

JOYCE: Originally they were all B.F.'s fish.

KARP: Old Butter Fingers.

P.H.: Karp . . . (*Pouring two glasses.*)

JOYCE: He used to sit for hours, staring into the tank.

P.H.: All the normal kids in the neighborhood preferred to watch
TV.

JOYCE: B.F. loved his fish. They were so mysterious to him. He'd
make up stories about them. Imagine they would jump out of the
tank at night, and while everyone else was asleep, they would do
all the chores that needed doing in the world. The heavy ones.
The impossible ones. The ones no one else could do.

P.H.: *It was those goddamn fish that ruined his life!*

JOYCE: Once I found him sitting naked in front of the tank. "Mama,"
he said, "imagine what it must be like to have water touching you
all over all the time!"

P.H.: An IQ close to genius.

BILL: What's he doing now?

JOYCE: He's a pearl diver.

BILL: No kidding! I used to do that.

JOYCE: You were a pearl diver?

BILL: Two years, almost.

JOYCE: In the Indian Ocean?

BILL: In Howard Johnson's.

JOYCE: Howard Johnson's?

BILL: I used to load the dishes into the machine.

JOYCE: They use dishes to dive for pearls now?

BILL: No, Ma'am, I was a dishwasher.

JOYCE: A dishwasher?

BILL: We're called pearl divers.

JOYCE: Why?

BILL: I don't rightly know. Because we bring the plates up white, I guess. (*Pause.* JOYCE *and* P.H. *exchange looks.*)

KARP: A dishwasher! (*Laughs.*) A goddamn dishwasher! (P.H. *blanches.*) Hey, Pat, we'll have to do a whole revision on that book! Dishes falling from the sky instead of pearls. The streets of New York covered with broken crockery. (*Laughs.* JOYCE *turns away from them.*)

BILL: I had one of the great experiences of my life washing dishes. (*They all look at him. Silence.*) This one time I was working pots and pans. Thinking about all the things I *really* wanted to do with my life. And there I was, in Howard Johnson's, up to my elbows in ooze and slime. All for two dollars and twenty-five cents an hour.

KARP: People get what they deserve.

BILL: Maybe. But there was a pressure in my chest told me I deserved a lot better. I was all set to tell them to shove their franchise, but I had this long history of quitting before finishing time, so I decided (*Snaps fingers.*) like that, to stick it out. At least till the end of the evening. The next few minutes were really hell. The pressure in here (*His chest.*) got so heavy, I thought I was gonna pass out. Then something in me rips. I mean I heard it rip. And all that weight lifts off. Then there's just me, and the sink, and my hands in the water, and the pots and pans banging together, and the whole kitchen throbbing like a kind of weird hive.

P.H.: (*Pause.*) And you call that one of the great experiences of your life?

BILL: Yeah.

P.H.: Some life.

JOYCE: Nothing like that ever happened to me. (*Silence.*)

KARP: So how come your old lady left you, Wild Bill?

JOYCE: That's none of your business, Bingo.

BILL: It's okay. I don't mind talking about it. I guess you could say our relationship was nothing but a series of uninterrupted irritations.

JOYCE: Even from the start?

BILL: (*Thinking this one.*) Yeah.

P.H.: What brought you together in the first place?

BILL: I was twenty-nine. Gettin' kinda tired of running around. When Janice came along, I was all primed up. Sometimes I think I would have married anyone, even a chimpanzee. Anyway, from the first date on, she gave me a hard time.

JOYCE: Maybe she didn't like being interchangeable with a chimpanzee.

BILL: I never told her she was interchangeable with a chimpanzee.

JOYCE: There are some things you don't have to tell a woman, Wild Bill.

KARP: As far as I'm concerned, pussy is the most overrated commodity on the market. (*Pause.*) Present company excepted, Joyce.

JOYCE: A woman wants to feel like she's one of a kind, Wild Bill.

P.H.: If all the rest of the ladies in the world are like you, Joyce, then, by god, every one of them is one of a kind!

JOYCE: What kind of a bad time did she give you?

BILL: We couldn't agree about anything.

KARP: How was your sex life?

BILL: That part of it was okay.

KARP: It was, huh?

P.H.: Would you be willing to take a lie detector test on that?

BILL: Janice used to say: "Hey, Filth, let's fight it out on our feet." Which meant, you know, we use the bed for what the bed should be used for. (*Pause.*) Anyway, everything was fine that way, till she started hounding me about a kid.

JOYCE: You didn't want a child?

BILL: (*Pause.*) No.

P.H.: Smart man.

JOYCE: Why not?

BILL: (*Pause.*) If we'd have had a kid, I'd have had to take them both on.

JOYCE: Both?

BILL: Yeah. She'd have had herself an ally. I mean, it would be no time at all before he was old enough to beat up on me. Then they'd get me on two fronts. Burn me down. Wear me out. I know what I'm talking about. My mom did the same with me. Kept sicking me on my dad. From the moment I'd hear his key in the lock, I was on him. "Daddy, gimme this, Daddy gimme that." Shit, I never let him have a moment's peace. One time I was sick, I saw this stupid commercial for whole wheat bread on TV. It's pouring outside, and I begin screaming I gotta have that bread. And the old man has to trek seventeen blocks in the rain, hitting every grocery till he brings it back And then, it's the lousiest bread I ever tasted, I can't even eat it. And then I wouldn't let him watch his favorite programs on TV. And wouldn't let him pick his nose, or sip his soup loud the way he liked. And once he fell asleep after dinner, I took a flying dive from across the room and landed both knees in his crotch.

JOYCE: Your mother told you to do all that?

BILL: Not in so many words.

P.H.: If old Butter Fingers ever tried anything like that on me, I'd have killed him on the spot!

JOYCE: And me, too, I suppose?

P.H.: You first!

BILL: Of course, Dad and I had some good times, too. When he started getting older, he'd drop by. We'd go for walks. Walks in the street. Walks in the park. Meet downtown for lunch. He'd tell me lots of crazy stuff about his childhood. Suddenly, he was full of stories. I forget them, now, most of them, but when he told them I had the feeling he wanted them remembered. He was tickled pink when I got married, too. Kept tellin' me to knock her up, or he would.

JOYCE: He was thinking about the future.

P.H.: The future . . .

KARP: Future's gonna be real ugly, Joyce. (*She looks at him.*) Crime.

JOYCE: When did she leave you, Wild Bill?

BILL: Last Sunday. I still don't understand it. We were havin' such a good time. We'd spent the afternoon in bed. Just kinda fell back in after we got up. Curtains in the bedroom are yellow, and the light through the window turned the whole room gold. There was a little breeze, too. And it was warm on our bodies. And there were kids on skateboards in the street. We were both lying there, looking up at the shadow of the fishtank. It was shimmering on the ceiling. And all the quick shadows of the fish, flashing on the walls between streaks of sunlight. "Hey, Filth," she says. "Look. Our kid is swimming on the ceiling."

JOYCE: Our kid is swimming on the ceiling . . .

KARP: Our kid is swimming on the ceiling?

BILL: "And that's the only place he's ever gonna swim, the bastard!" says I. Well, that's when the shit hit the fan. There's a moment of silence. Then she gives me a shove. She's out of bed, dressing, packing her bags. She wouldn't talk or give me the time of day. I kept saying, "What's the matter, sweetheart. Let's negotiate this."

KARP: (*Belches.*) I don't feel so good. (*Rises.*)

P.H.: Too much juice, Bingo?

KARP: Too much cake. 'Scuse me all a moment. (*He exits to bathroom.*)

JOYCE: What happened then, Wild Bill?

BILL: Nothing more to tell. She left in a real huff, holding on to her breath the same way you do, Ma'am.

JOYCE: Holding on to her breath?

BILL: Though she only holds it when she's angry, whereas I noticed you hold yours all the time.

JOYCE: (*Quite surprised.*) I hold my breath all the time?

BILL: Yeah. Every time you inhale, you (*He demonstrates holding his breath.*) hold your breath like someone was gonna hit you hard or drop a big rock on your head. (*He lets his breath go.*) Then you let it go. (JOYCE *lets her breath go.*) Like that. All in a rush. (*He demonstrates again, holds, lets breath go in a rush.*)

JOYCE: But I've always breathed that way. (*Holds, lets her breath go.*) I've breathed that way ever since I was little. (*Holds, lets breath go.*)

P.H.: It's true. Half the time she sounds like her lungs are constipated.

JOYCE: (*Holding, letting go.*) Are you trying to tell me I've been breathing all wrong?

BILL: Right or wrong isn't the issue. You're not getting as much oxygen as you might if you . . . (*He breathes, establishing a regular rhythm.*) You see what I mean? (*He demonstrates the right way to breathe. She imitates, the two of them breathing together. Off,* BINGO *heaving up his guts.*)

P.H.: I think Bingo's in a bit of trouble.

BILL: In and out, Ma'am. (*Demonstrates; she imitates.*) Try to get the rhythm even. (*They breathe together.*)

Peter Coyote (BILL) *and Linda Hoy* (JOYCE) *in the Magic Theatre production.*

JOYCE: In and out . . .

BILL: Don't talk. Just breathe. (*He breathes. She breathes.*)

JOYCE: Breathe.

BILL: Feel the difference?

JOYCE: Um.

P.H.: Hey, Karp! You all right? (BINGO, *heaving.* BILL *and* JOYCE *breathing.*) Joyce, you're turning as red as a beet.

JOYCE: It's all right, P.H.. I'm just breathing.

BILL: Good. (JOYCE *breathing.*) That's terrific.

JOYCE: (*Laughing.*) It's making me feel (*Breathes.*) giddy. (*Breathing, laughing, catching her air.*) Oh.

P.H.: What have you got her doing, there?

BILL: Breathing.

P.H.: I thought you were a car mechanic!

BILL: I am.

P.H.: So what's this physical therapy you're performing on my wife?

BILL: It's no therapy. She's just getting more oxygen.

JOYCE: More oxygen! (*Sound of* BINGO *heaving.*)

P.H.: Hey, Bingo!

JOYCE: More oxygen! It is a substance, isn't it?

BILL: Breathe.

JOYCE: Breathe. Yes. Once on an airplane trip to visit my parents in Florida . . .

BILL: Breathe.

JOYCE: Breathe. I looked out the window. I could see the thickness of the air.

BILL: Breathe.

JOYCE: (*Breathing.*) I could see it. The air. Like an ocean. Thick. Rolling over the earth. (*Breathing.*) And that's what I'm breathing now. That thickness!

BILL: Breathe.

JOYCE: I'm filling up on it! (*Breathes.*) Oh. Oh. Oh. My head is spinning. I'm lifting off like a balloon. (*She reels, begins to fall.* BILL *catches her.*) Oh.

BILL: Easy.

JOYCE: Wild Bill.

BILL: Breathe.

JOYCE: (*She breathes; her whole body catches in a sob.*) Oh. (*She shudders, curls up on herself.*) Oh.

P.H.: Hey, what's going on now? Joyce?

JOYCE: Oh.

P.H.: What is it?

JOYCE: Pain. Oh. Oh. Pain. In my stomach. All over. (*Sobbing.*)

P.H.: What the hell have you done to my wife! Get away from her! (BILL *lets her sit on the floor, moves off.* P.H. *hovers.*) Joyce? Come on, now, Joyce. You're all right.

JOYCE: I'm not all right. (*Breathing.*)

P.H.: Joyce . . .

JOYCE: Don't touch me! (*Breathing.*)

P.H.: Hey, Karp!

KARP: (*Enters, breathing hard.*) Yeah. I'm okay. What's going on? What's Joyce doing on the floor?

P.H.: This sonofabitch is practicing therapy without a license!

KARP: Hey, Joyce?

JOYCE: (*Breathing, into herself.*) All wrong. Since I was little. Breathing all wrong. I might have been a completely different person. (*Breathing, sobs.*)

KARP: Hey, Joyce. Do you know me? It's me, Bingo. (*She breathes.*) Your toilet's stopped up.

JOYCE: (*Pulls herself away, half crawls, until she's in her own free space.*) A completely different person. (*Deep breaths.*) Other things would have happened to me. Things that never happened to me. (*Breathing.*)

KARP: What's she talking about?

P.H.: She doesn't like it here.

JOYCE: Other voices than the same old voices, telling me what I can do, what I can't do.

KARP: What voices? (*To* P.H.) She hears voices?

P.H.: This is the first I ever heard of it. (JOYCE *shudders; a low guttural cry of disgust.*) Jesus!

KARP: Careful, Pat. Something's really wrong there.

P.H.: Joyce . . .

JOYCE: Telling me there would be certain days of the year set aside for special events! Special events! A trip day, an assembly day, a guest speaker. And you prepare, you prepare for something different. Confirmation. Graduation. My first period. My first kiss. (*Shudders.*) They all want you to believe there's something out there that's yours and yours alone. (*Looking at her hands.*) Like Miss Samuelson in the fourth grade telling us all about our fingerprints. How our fingerprints were all different and how that difference made each one of us unique.

KARP: (*Banging table.*) Fingerprints are unique, goddamnit!

JOYCE: Or like snowflakes.

P.H.: Snowflakes?

JOYCE: Each single snowflake falling just once to earth, then melting away with billions of others . . .

KARP: So what?

JOYCE: *Exactly! So what?* (*Looks around.*) I haven't got anything that's really mine!

P.H.: What about your fish?

JOYCE: My fish? (*She grabs the bottle from table, rushes tank with it, upraised, like club.*) I'll smash that tank to pieces!

KARP: (*Grabbing her.*) Whoa! Grab her, Pat! (*Both men restrain her.*)

JOYCE: I'll smash it!

P.H.: And you do, your fish will die, Joyce!

JOYCE: Good! I want them *all* to die!

P.H.: That's wicked, Joyce! It's irresponsible!

JOYCE: *I don't care! I want them all to die!*

P.H.: (*Shaking her.*) Joyce!

BILL: For Chrissake, let her be!

P.H.: You shut up! If you hadn't started her breathing, none of this would have happened! (*Pause.* JOYCE *is still.* P.H. *lets her go. She remains, staring before her, as though listening.*) Joyce?

JOYCE: Shhhhh.

P.H.: What's happening?

JOYCE: Shhh. (*Listening.*) B.F. . . .

P.H.: B.F.?

JOYCE: (*Listens.*) "Mommy, I love you. I love you, Mommy." Like when he was five. Kissing. Climbing over my lap and shoulders. "Mommy, I want to marry you."

P.H.: Jesus!

KARP: A good thing he split when he did.

JOYCE: I wanted to name him Terrence. A real name. How could he ever trust me, letting him go into the world with a name like Benjamin Franklin! It's like having no name at all!

P.H.: Listen, Joyce, there's something . . .

JOYCE: And now he's out there, somewhere, with nothing to remember me by but the holding of my breath. He's out there, holding his own breath and groping from one blind moment to another.

P.H.: He's not groping, Joyce. He's washing dishes.

JOYCE: With only the dream of a pearl to light his way.

P.H.: (*Softly.*) Someone else's dishes.

JOYCE: Where am I? What place is this?

P.H.: This is your home, Joyce.

JOYCE: No. This is not my home.

P.H.: You think you're the only one around here carrying a burden!

KARP: Maybe the two of you should spend this Easter in Hawaii.

JOYCE: It's not my home! (*Breathing.*) Wild Bill!

BILL: Yes, Ma'am?

JOYCE: What you've done is wrong!

BILL: Wrong?

JOYCE: What you've done is wrong, wrong, wrong!

BILL: What have I done?

JOYCE: You drove your wife away!

BILL: I didn't drive her. She left.

JOYCE: And now you'll live by yourself, with nothing but the fish for company, and it's all wrong!

KARP: What's wrong? I live by myself, and I don't even have any fish.

JOYCE: That's you, Bingo! You can live that way because you're not a passionate soul!

KARP: I'm not what?

JOYCE: But you, Wild Bill, you are a passionate soul!

BILL: I am?

JOYCE: Yes! And a passionate soul cannot hope to survive with only fish for company! (*Wildly, tearfully.*) Take my word for it! A passionate soul needs someone real to talk to!

KARP: Who says I'm not a passionate soul, Joyce?

JOYCE: Was she real, Wild Bill?

BILL: Yeah.

JOYCE: And you do miss her?

BILL: Yeah . . .

KARP: Pat, you've known me for years. Would you say I'm a passionate soul?

P.H.: Without a doubt, Bingo. You are a passionate soul.

JOYCE: And don't you think she misses you?

BILL: I donno.

JOYCE: Oh Wild Bill, why do you suppose she left her fish?

BILL: The tank's much too heavy.

JOYCE: No! Because it's something she loves.

BILL: Loves?

JOYCE: Something she wants to come back to!

KARP: Joyce, you don't know me well enough to say I'm not a passionate soul!

JOYCE: Oh, hush, I'm talking to Wild Bill! Why don't you phone
her?

BILL: Phone her?

JOYCE: You know where she is?

BILL: Her brother's.

KARP: The fact is, you don't know me at all, Joyce! (*To* P.H.) She
doesn't know me.

P.H.: Don't take it personally, Bingo. She doesn't know me, either.

JOYCE: There's an extension in the kitchen. You can have privacy.

BILL: Yeah, well, I donno. I miss her, true. But then again, it's been
awfully peaceful round the house.

JOYCE: And it'll be more peaceful in the grave, Wild Bill!

P.H.: What suddenly qualifies you to be this man's marriage coun-
selor?

JOYCE: Oxygen!

KARP: Well, I have something to say about passion, goddamnit!
Those who know me on the job know I'm a passionate soul!

P.H.: (*To* JOYCE.) You've really offended that man, Joyce!

KARP: And those who know me off the job know I'm a passionate
soul!

P.H.: (*To* JOYCE.) You owe Bingo an apology.

KARP: Nah, nah, nah, she doesn't owe me anything! I could tell you
lotsa stories about my passion, Joyce. But I don't have to prove
nothing to you! All the same, I'd like you to know a little something about me and Gloria!

P.H.: Gloria?

KARP: I never told you about Gloria, did I, Pat?

P.H.: No, Bingo, you did not.

KARP: She was a cocktail waitress! A real dish! Great in bed! *And*
passionate!

P.H.: How come you never mentioned her?

KARP: She was too disturbed to talk about!

P.H.: In what way was she disturbed, Bingo?

KARP: Every time we'd finish making love, she'd cry. "What's wrong,
sweetheart?" "I donno," she'd wail. But I knew. She slept on this
king-sized bed, an' all night long she'd fight in her sleep. Twist
and turn and moan and four mornings out of seven she'd end up
on the floor. "Who is it you're fighting with," I'd ask her. "I
donno," she'd say. "Marry me, Bingo." "Sweetheart, you are too
disturbed to marry. Why don't you reconcile yourself to the fact
you are great in bed and stop worrying so much about getting

married?" And she'd give me this look. Anyway we went together for a year, and then we broke up.

BILL: Excuse me, Ma'am. I think after all I will use your phone.

JOYCE: In the kitchen!

BILL: Thanks!

JOYCE: You take your time, Wild Bill! And good luck! He's gone
in to call his wife! (*She breathes.*)

KARP: I haven't finished my story, Joyce.

JOYCE: What story?

P.H.: Jesus.

KARP: My story about Gloria.

P.H.: Just tell *me* your story, Bingo.

KARP: I want Joyce to hear this story, Pat.

P.H.: Joyce is breathing. But she's listening, too, aren't you, Joyce?

JOYCE: Yes, I'm listening. Go on with your story, Bingo.

KARP: Okay. A couple of years pass. One day I see her again. In
Zim's. She's looking better than ever. My heart goes thump. But
she's with this fruity-looking guy, limp wrists and all the rest of
it. He turns out to be a sandal maker.

P.H.: A sandal maker?

KARP: Yeah. She lifts her foot. "Paul made these." Shows me her
whole calf and thigh and this guy's sandal. "How nice," I say. And
then I bid her goodbye. But all that night, I can't get those san-
dals out of my head. They're right on her feet. Hugging her feet.
Wound round her feet. And this fruity guy made them. And she's
like living in the nest he stitched together. And the thought drives
me crazy. So I get on the phone at two in the morning, and I tell
her how great it was to see her again. And how I missed her. And
how I'd like to get together as soon as possible and talk about the
future. "Come on over," she says. "Come on over, you sweetheart!" (*Pause.*)

P.H.: What happened, then?

KARP: What do you think? A half hour later we're screwing like
panthers. And just as soon as we get into it, I go right for her
feet. Squeezing and kissing and pressing my forehead to them,
and my chest, and every other part of my body . . . (BILL *enters.*)

JOYCE: Here's Wild Bill! My god, what'd she say?

BILL: She's coming home!

JOYCE: Oh, wonderful! (*An impulsive hug.*)

BILL: (*Clumsy.*) Yeah . . .

KARP: Doesn't anyone want to hear the end of my story?

P.H.: I do, Bingo. Go on. I'm listening.

JOYCE: I want to hear the end of Wild Bill's story! Go on, Bill! (*She breathes.*)

BILL: Well, first thing I did, I dialed her number.

JOYCE: Yes?

BILL: The tone rings three times.

JOYCE: Yes?

BILL: The receiver goes click and she says, "Okay, identify yourself!"

JOYCE: Identify yourself, yes?

BILL: "Hi, Mouse, it's me."

JOYCE: Mouse?

BILL: I always call her "Mouse," on account of she's afraid of everything.

JOYCE: How sweet. He calls her Mouse.

BILL: "Hi, Mouse. It's me, Mr. Filth."

JOYCE: (*Gasps, breathes, laughs.*) Mouse. Mr. Filth. It's beautiful.

BILL: Yeah.

JOYCE: So what'd she say?

BILL: She don't say nothing. It's like death on the other end of the line.

JOYCE: Yes?

BILL: Then I said, "What'cha been doin', Mouse?" "King Tut," she says.

JOYCE: King Tut?

P.H.: King Tut?

BILL: "I'm sitting on the floor, doin' this gigantic jigsaw puzzle of the Golden Funeral Mask of King Tut."

JOYCE: Ohhhhhh. The Golden Funeral Mask.

BILL: "How far you got, Mouse?" "Far enough," she says. "If you hadn't called before I got his nose in, I was gonna sue you for divorce." Well, that starts me laughing like hell. "So what makes you so sure you know the object of this call?" I say. Then she laughs. "Don't take anything for granted, Filth, 'cause I may sue you anyway." So I say, "The goddamn fish sure miss you." And she says, "Fuck the fish. I'm pregnant." (JOYCE *breathes.*) So I says, "You sure don't waste any time."

JOYCE: She's pregnant!

BILL: And I says, "Am I the father?"

JOYCE: And she says?

BILL: "Whoever teaches him to swim is the father."

JOYCE: Whoever teaches . . . ?

BILL: And I says, "I'll teach him." And she says, "Okay, you're the father."

JOYCE: You're the father!

BILL: So I'm gonna pick her up in ten minutes in the tow truck.

JOYCE: (*Gives him a hug.*) Oh, Wild Bill!

P.H.: Think you got time to give my goddamn battery a charge before you go?

BILL: Hell, yes! That's what I came for, isn't it?

P.H. You had me wondering. Come on!

They exit through glass door.

JOYCE: Whoever teaches him to swim . . .

KARP: All that happened over sixteen years ago.

JOYCE: All what?

KARP: Nothing. Forget it.

JOYCE: Don't you think it's wonderful, Bingo?

KARP: What?

JOYCE: Wild Bill and his Mouse are getting back together again.

KARP: Yeah, it's just great, Joyce.

JOYCE: It is.

KARP: Joyce? (*She breathes.*) Joyce, there's something I think you and me have to get straight.

JOYCE: What's that, Bingo?

KARP: If I'm gonna come and go in this house, I'm gonna have to have more respect.

JOYCE: (*Breathing.*) Who from, Bingo?

KARP: From you, goddamnit! (*Pause.* JOYCE *breathes.* BINGO *grabs, tries to kiss her.*)

JOYCE: Bingo! Bingo Karp! What are you dooooooing! Mmmmmm-mmmmffffffph! Bingmmmmmmmmmmmufpf! Stop! Stop it! Bingo! (*They wrestle.*) Have you lost your mind?

KARP: You've only yourself to blame, Joyce. You've driven me to it! (*He embraces her again.*)

JOYCE: Enough! Bingo! P.H. will be coming back!

KARP: Fuck P.H.!

JOYCE: He's your best friend.

KARP: P.H.? That man and I have absolutely nothing in common. I'll tell you the truth about P.H., Joyce. He lacks integrity. (*Squeezes, kisses her.*)

JOYCE: But you call him your friend! (*Pushing him off.*)

KARP: He lacks integrity! (*Checks out window.*) He's coming back. I wouldn't mention this if I were you. He has a weak heart. (*Silence.* KARP *pours from the bottle into glass. Drinks. Sits.* P.H. *enters.*) Well, how's it going, old buddy? You get that battery charged?

P.H.: Yeah.

JOYCE: Where's Wild Bill?

P.H.: He's doing something in his truck.

JOYCE: He'll be coming back to the house, won't he? (*Silence.*)

KARP: What's the matter with you, Pat? You look as white as a ghost.

P.H.: I've got to sit down.

KARP: You all right, Pat?

P.H.: I feel a little funny. Something happened in the garage.

JOYCE: It's not your heart, is it?

P.H.: There's a pressure there. (*Feels his heart.*) It's beating very fast.

KARP: Does he have medicine?

P.H.: I just took my medicine. Maybe another pill or two.

KARP: Joyce, where's his medicine?

JOYCE: In the bathroom.

KARP: Go get it.

JOYCE: Yes. (*She exits.*)

KARP: Pat . . .

P.H.: Yeah . . .

KARP: I have something to confess to you.

P.H.: What?

KARP: Nothing. How do you feel?

P.H.: I donno. Funny. I think I blacked out in the garage. I was looking at him, bent over like he was. Half of him under the hood, the cables twisted. (*Breathing hard.*) And it annoyed me, to see him like that.

KARP: Like what?

P.H.: Bent over, half gone under the hood. Then I couldn't breathe. All of a sudden, I had no air. I felt like I was drowning. I started toward him. Everything reeled. Bingo! (*Breathing hard.*)

KARP: Pat?

P.H.: I don't want to die!

KARP: Hey, buddy. No one's gonna die around here. You'll live to bury us all.

P.H.: I hope so.

Linda Hoy (JOYCE) *and Rick Prindle* (KARP) *in the Magic Theatre production.*

KARP: Hey, Joyce . . .

JOYCE: I'm coming . . .

P.H.: Bingo . . .

KARP: Pat?

P.H.: You believe I'm really ill now?

KARP: (*Nods.*) Sure, Pat.

P.H.: Bingo . . . (*Motions* BINGO *to lean in.*)

KARP: I'm right here, Pat.

P.H.: Your breath stinks.

KARP: My breath . . . (*Sniffs.*)

JOYCE: (*Entering with bottle and water.*) Here's the medicine.

KARP: Okay, old buddy, swallow these. Swallow and drink, old buddy. (P.H. *takes pills, water.*) Joyce?

JOYCE: Yes?

KARP: You got any gauze in the house?

JOYCE: Gauze?

KARP: I need some gauze.

JOYCE: What for?

KARP: It's important!

JOYCE: Gauze? In the bathroom, maybe.

KARP: Could you look?

JOYCE: Yes. (*She exits.*)

P.H.: What do you need gauze for, Bingo?

KARP: I just wanted to keep her busy while I tell you something.

P.H.: What?

KARP: (*Pause.*) If anything happens to you, Pat, I want you to know I'll look after Joyce.

P.H.: Thanks, Bingo. But there's another favor you can do me.

KARP: Name it.

P.H.: You know the Swedish Baths on Broadway Avenue?

KARP: Yeah.

P.H.: There's a masseuse there named Raiko.

KARP: Raiko, the little Japanese girl?

P.H.: Yeah.

KARP: What about her, Pat?

P.H.: Tell her, "Thanks." (*Pause.*)

JOYCE: (*Enters.*) I've found the gauze.

KARP: Great. Now what I want you to do, Joyce, I want you to take this gauze outside. (*Pointing to yard.*) There's that beautiful tree . . . You know the one I'm talking about?

JOYCE: The one that's been out there for twenty-three years, Bingo?

KARP: That's the one!

JOYCE: Yes!

KARP: I want you to wind this roll of gauze around it.

JOYCE: Wind this gauze around the oak tree?

KARP: Slowly. Very slowly.

JOYCE: Why?

KARP: I'll tell you why when you've finished.

JOYCE: I'd like to know why now.

P.H.: *Can't you for once in your life do as you're told!*

JOYCE: *Why are you shouting at me?*

P.H.: *Because I'm a sick man! (Pause.* JOYCE *turns, exits into yard.)*

KARP: Thanks, Pat. I didn't feel it incumbent on my part to yell at her. (JOYCE, *visible through the glass, stands in front of tree, the box of gauze in her hand.*) Women! Goddamn women! (JOYCE *opens box, removes roll of gauze, looks at it, looks at tree. Looks back at house.* BINGO *makes "wind it around" motions.* JOYCE *turns, looks at tree.*)

P.H.: Is she bandaging the tree?

KARP: She's working into it.

P.H.: God, what a fool!

KARP: (*Looks over at him.*) Why'd you marry her?

P.H.: Because she knew more about the Mafia than anyone else in the world. (JOYCE *is leaning against the tree.*) What's she doing now?

KARP: She's embracing the tree.

P.II.: (*Turns his head to see.*) Christ.

KARP: I think she's crying.

P.H.: That's their goddamn solution to everything.

KARP: Yeah. (*Pause.*) So what's going on between you and that Japanese masseuse? (P.H. *Laughs.* JOYCE *lifts herself off the tree, unwinds a span of gauze, holds it pressed against the trunk.*) You know, Pat, I sometimes wonder if you are as sincere in this friendship of ours as I am.

> P.H. *laughs.* KARP, *very serious, stares at him. A smile breaks over his face.* P.H. *laughs harder.* KARP *giggles. The two men explode with laughter. It subsides. They look at each other, simultaneously explode again.* KARP *raises one hand, thumb on nose, waves all his other fingers, making fart-like sound.* P.H. *returns the same with both hands. Like boys, they give over completely to the open-ended, indefinable ambiguity of their situation.*

JOYCE, *meanwhile, trying to transfer the roll of gauze from one hand to the other around the tree, finds the trunk too thick. Her hands don't meet. She begins to circle the tree slowly, clockwise. At the end of one of* P.H. *and* KARP's *explosions, only* JOYCE's *hands, trying to pass the gauze, are visible.* KARP *calls* P.H.'s *attention to the sight.* JOYCE *gives the roll a little toss, catching it and so effecting the first complete circle. The men explode with renewed hilarity.* KARP *pours the last of the bottle into two glasses.* JOYCE *continues, now, slowly to wind gauze around tree.*

KARP: Patrick Henry Bibbs! (*Lifts glass.*)

P.H.: Yeah, old buddy...

KARP: While you were out in the garage, doing whatever you were doing... (*Laughs.*)

P.H.: (*Laughing.*) Yeah?

KARP: Your wife propositioned me! Cheers! (*He drinks.*)

P.H.: (*No laugh.*)

KARP: It wasn't the first time either. (P.H. *gives a moan, his hand to his heart.*) I've been fighting off that woman's advances since the day you introduced us. (P.H. *is breathing very hard.*) I never touched her, though. Scout's Honor. If I never said anything about it to date, it was because I hoped this insane passion of hers would pass, and she'd settle down with you like the good woman you must have thought you married. But it never happened, Pat. She would phone me in the middle of the night. Ask me to recommend her books on the Mafia to read. The more I spurned her, the crazier and wilder her passion for me became.

P.H.: Bingo...

KARP: Yeah, Pat?

P.H.: Why are you telling me all this now?

KARP: Because I fear for you, Pat. There's something unreal about your whole existence.

P.H.: Unreal? (*They stare at each other.*)

KARP: Yeah. Unreal. It's not your fault. It's her.

P.H.: Her? (*They both look through window.* JOYCE *is slowly winding gauze around tree.*)

KARP: It's what marriage does to a man.

P.H.: Marriage! (JOYCE *winds gauze around tree.*)

KARP: S'like a fog, Pat. A fog a man wanders into, never to be heard or seen again. And women secrete it. In the name of some godless passion, they secrete it. Look at her out there, secreting fog. Have you any idea at all what's really going on in her mind?

(JOYCE, *coming to end of bandage, tucks it in.*)

P.H.: No.

KARP: Better, I say, never to know. (JOYCE *turns slowly, looking at them.*)

P.H.: She doesn't really belong to this world, does she?

KARP: Neither to this world, Pat, nor to any other.

JOYCE *raises her hand, bursts out laughing. In response to her gesture, an undersea chord, echoing. The lights blink off. Another set of lights blinks on: blue, red, green. A huge column of bubbles rises from floor to ceiling, rear, as the entire stage is transformed into a gigantic aquarium, full of watery shadows.*

KARP *and* P.H. *move about like two strange fish. They make "boh-boh" sounds, use their arms like fins, their bodies lifted and jostled by the new thickness of the environment.*

The undersea chord, heard over and over again. It is full of muffled cheering voices, growing louder.

A diver in an old-fashioned diving suit is slowly lowered from above. He makes his way, followed by P.H. *and* BINGO, *searching the various parts of the house, looking under cushions, in cupboards, drawers, the oven, icebox, etc. Finally, in nook, or closet, uncovers, in hat box, a huge egg-shaped pearl. It glows, throwing a weird radiance over everything. Muffled cheering.*

JOYCE *moves in, presses her hands and nose against the glass wall.*

P.H. *and* KARP *move about, slow motion. They circle diver, butting, sniffing the pearl.* P.H. *lifts it, carries it away. He tosses it to* KARP. *Chord. Cheering. Diver moves after* KARP, *who tosses it back to* P.H.. *Balloon-like, it floats through space. Chord. Cheering. Diver moves after* P.H., *who tosses it back to* KARP. *Chord. Cheering. Diver moves into the center. As* KARP *passes, diver mounts chair and leaps, rising into space. He intercepts the pearl, winding his arms around it. He and the pearl sink slowly to the stage.*

P.H. *and* KARP *close in.* KARP *draws revolver.* P.H. *picks up cake knife. They make menacing faces. While* KARP *pulls at diver,* P.H. *cuts the air line. Bubbles. Diver releases pearl, begins to writhe and gag.* P.H. *and* KARP, *off to side with pearl. Diver writhes, drowns.* P.H. *over to prostrate floating form, stabs it, comes back, grabs egg. Smears it with blood. Accompanying chords. Cheering. Lights dim. Only the pearl now giving off any illumination.* P.H. *and* KARP *hover and struggle for it.* P.H. *brandishes knife.* KARP *fires revolver.*

Complete darkness.

Chord. One voice, JOYCE's, *sobbing.*

The lights come up, slowly. The scene is the same as before.
KARP, *looking out into the yard.* JOYCE, *looking in, hands and
nose pressed to glass.* P.H., *in chair, his hand over his heart.
Silence.*

KARP: She's looking right at us, but she doesn't see us. (*He hits the
glass with his fist.* JOYCE *lifts herself off, looks at him, turns her face
away, remains motionless.*) Pat?
P.H.: Hm?
KARP: It's probably best not to mention I told you anything.
P.H.: Told me what?
KARP: All that stuff about Joyce. She'll only deny it. They're all
liars, you know. Not even aware they're lying. The only thing we
men can do is keep them busy. Keep them busy and meet their
lies with silence. Yes. The old silent treatment. You hear me,
Pat?
P.H.: Hm?
KARP: (*Whispers.*) Give me liberty or give me . . . (*Finger to lips.*)
Shhhh. (JOYCE *slides door open, enters. Silence.*) Well, Joyce, how'd
it go out there? (*Silence.*) I see you bandaged the tree. You see
the way she bandaged the tree, Pat? (*Pause.*) And did a terrific
job, too. Didn't she do a terrific job, Pat? Turned that tree into a
work of art, almost. (*Pause.*) Joyce, you turned that tree into a
work of art. Almost. (*Silence.*) Well, the bottle's empty. I think I
will be moving on. (*Takes his jacket.*) Shouldn't keep the professor waiting. Seeing as I'm his brother, right? Pat? (*Extends hand
for a handshake.* P.H. *looks at him, doesn't move.*) Joyce . . . (*Moves
his hand toward her. She looks at him, doesn't move. He lowers his
hand.*) Well, I never did put too much faith in a handshake my-
self. Spreads germs. (*Pause.*) I'll show myself out. (*He exits, right.
Silence.*)
JOYCE: I never want that man to set foot in this house again. (*Pause,
as though waking.*) Where's Wild Bill?
P.H.: He's dead.
JOYCE: Dead?
P.H.: Washed away by a wave.
JOYCE: What are you talking about?
P.H.: B.F.
JOYCE: (*At door, slides it open.*) Wild Bill!
P.H.: (*To himself.*) No future at all to speak of.
JOYCE: (*Softly.*) Wild Bill . . .

From behind the tree, BILL *appears. Enters the house.*

BILL: The battery's charged. Though I'd drive it about an hour if you want the charge to last. (*With clipboard.*) You all right, Bibbs? Your husband blacked out for a moment in the garage.

JOYCE: Wild Bill . . .

BILL: Yes, Ma'am? (JOYCE *nods, turns away, catches her breath.*) You can sign this. (*Gives clipboard to* P.H.)

P.H.: What is it?

BILL: The repair form. To show I was here. And did something for your car. (P.H. *signs form. Hands the clipboard to him.*) I wanted to thank you, Ma'am, and let you know whatever happens now between Janice and me, you're always gonna own a little piece of it. (*He gives her an impulsive hug. She backs away, turns, holds her breath.*) What's your wife's name?

P.H.: Joyce.

BILL: Hey, Joyce? (*She turns around. Pause. He extends his finger, pinning the command on her.*) Breathe! (*She breathes. To* P.H.) *The Declaration of Independence* was written by Thomas Jefferson. Check it out. (*He exits.*)

P.H.: (*Sliding door closed.*) I've a good mind to report that bastard! I called him up to do a simple job. (JOYCE *sits, cries, trying to breathe.*) How long you going to keep that wheezing up? You sound like a goddamn iron lung!

JOYCE: (*She softens the tone of her breathing, sustains its regularity.*) Why'd you tell me he'd been washed away by a wave?

P.H.: I don't know.

JOYCE: I have a feeling something's happened to him myself.

P.H.: Who?

JOYCE: B.F. His life isn't turning out as it should.

P.H.: Whose life does?

JOYCE: But why?

P.H.: Why what?

JOYCE: Why shouldn't people's lives turn out better?

P.H.: I don't know. (*She cries, soft. He stares at her, away.*) I miss him, too. Sometimes. Together with my father. I miss them both, sometimes. Sometimes I get them confused, in my sleep. I dream I'm in the bathroom, looking in the mirror. It's B.F. looking back at me, or my father. We're making faces at each other. Funny faces sometimes. Sometimes serious faces. Very serious faces. Then he turns his back. B.F. or my father. Turns his back and disappears. And I'm left looking at nothing. No image at all in the glass. For a moment, I don't know where I am. Then, I pick up my toothbrush, spread some paste. Pretend like nothing's happened. (*They look at each other.*) I'd better see to the car. (*He exits.*)

JOYCE *sits, looks front, breathes.*

The lights dim. Hum of aquarium up. JOYCE *in glow of aquarium, together with tree, mysteriously illuminated by the same source.*

JOYCE *exhales. Aquarium light off.*

CURTAIN